EASY AND DELICIOUS

VEGAN RECIPES FOR BUSY PEOPLE

Everyday Vegan

EASY AND DELICIOUS

VEGAN RECIPES FOR BUSY PEOPLE

Everyday Vegan

Jackie Norman & Gareth Scurr

NEW HOLLAND

Contents

Acknowledgements

This book would not have been possible without the help and kindness of the following people and groups, who opened their homes and their hearts to enable us to make it happen:

Sharon Aston

Bronwen Hallam

Michael and Irene Leonard

Christina Scurr

Brent and Liz Waterhouse

Mike and Liz Williams

Peter Webber and Ann Norman

The Riches Have Wheels Community – We got there!

Massive thanks to Angel Foods, who have backed us from the very start. Thank you for your amazing support and service, for all the care packages, and for making it easier and more delicious for people to be vegan.

We would also like to thank the following for the part they have played in this journey, even if they didn't know it:

Tiana Jade Howe – for sowing the first seed.

Robyn Irons – for making it burst into life.

And last, but definitely not least, we would like to dedicate this book to Slade Julian. Forever famous for his love of food and for dreaming up crazy dishes, we will keep doing our best to create amazing things to eat. You may not have been vegan, in this lifetime or the next. In fact, you probably couldn't have thought of anything worse! But we will always love you anyway.

Introduction

– *Cooking with Joy*

When I first made the decision to go vegan, my mother said, 'Jackie you can't do that! I'll kill you!' Honestly, she said those exact words. Like many people, she thought her beloved daughter would fade away into a shadow, existing on nothing but a waft of lettuce leaves and a pocketful of goji berries. While Gareth and I didn't think things would be that dire, we did expect to lose at least half our body weight and be constantly hungry. How wrong we all were.

From Day One, the two of us launched into a culinary journey. The mundane chore of cooking immediately became an exciting, new, daily adventure, sparking a whole new love of food. Never in a million years did we think cooking and eating plants would ever bring so much variety, so much *joy*. It was this joy we wanted to share, right from the outset, so we began a Facebook page – 'Camper Van Kitchen' – where we could share recipes and our newfound culinary passion. The other main reason for starting that page, was because we wanted to demonstrate how easy it is to cook and eat well while still being vegan. At the time, we were living on the road permanently, travelling the length and breadth of the country in a 4.6-metre-long camper van. Our entire kitchen was just a metre wide and every dish we made was on a two-burner portable hob. We earned less in a month than most people did in a week, yet we were cooking and eating better now than we ever had in our lives. The main challenge we faced as new vegans was being based in a rural town. There were only three vegans in the whole place, and we were two of them. With no access to many of the mythical wonders we were reading about, such as tempeh and seitan, we had no choice but to cook everything completely from scratch – using everyday things from the supermarket. This was the best thing that could have happened however, as we learned to cook *real* food, using *real* ingredients, right from the start.

We also learned vegan food didn't have to be expensive. If you rely on mainly processed and ready-made vegan foods, then yes, it can be an expensive way to eat. A lot of emphasis is placed these days on 'loaded' foods and the latest products, but that isn't our style. We don't want to spend a fortune stacking our food up to excess in order to make it taste good, and we don't want anyone else to have to either. This book isn't going to have you buying forests of kale to pulverise into a smoothie, or furiously blending cashews to make into a sauce. Our recipes are designed to be as easy and as low-cost as possible, while helping to solve a lot of common problems. These include:

Quick 'no brain' meals to feed the family when you're tired

Kid-friendly foods, plus clever ideas to sneak more good stuff into picky eaters

Lunch inspiration, for home and at work

'Blokey' foods, that will appeal to and satisfy the biggest appetites

Food that travels well, to save you money and hassle when out and about

Food to share with friends, that both vegans and non-vegans will love

Food for special occasions, when you need to pull out all the stops, impress a date or feed a crowd

Unapologetically indulgent foods, for when you want to pamper yourself or a loved one

This book also caters for various food allergies and intolerances, which we live with ourselves every day. These can be stressful, especially in families and social situations, so we have taken some of the hard work out of wondering what is safe to cook by labelling each recipe at the start, so you know at a glance.

To give you an idea, Gareth can eat everything but I'm coeliac *and* also can't eat grains. I can't tolerate garlic, onion and many other high FODMAP foods, either. This made developing many of our recipes interesting, especially when I was diagnosed halfway through creating this book! In all honesty though, it turned out to be a blessing in disguise. As a result, almost every recipe has now been tailored to make it safe for as many people as possible, wherever possible. As the many people who cannot eat alliums (onions, garlic, chives, shallots, spring onions and leeks) will tell you, they are in pretty much *everything*. But just as we learned when we stopped eating meat, eggs and dairy, you can make things taste truly delicious without alliums too. Changing the *way* we cook and eat has enabled us to break away from the usual trends and the belief that everything always needs garlic or onion. This doesn't mean however, that you can't add them if you would prefer. Of course you can!

Home cooking is without a doubt the best, cheapest and easiest way to make sure everything you eat is safe, without having to worry about scrutinising labels, or feeling

 FODMAPS are 'fermentable oligo-, di-, mono-saccharides and polyols' – short-chain carbohydrates that some people find hard to digest, causing gas, bloating and other unpleasantness in susceptible individuals.'

embarrassed in restaurants for having to ask a million questions. Vegan options are becoming more readily available in cafes and restaurants by the day, and there is nothing nicer than stumbling upon a tiny place in the middle of nowhere and discovering they offer vegan food. However, dining out when vegan can still be terribly frustrating. Our recipes are for everyone who gets fed up of having to order hot chips and a plain side salad. We're here for all those who have been charged the full price for a restaurant meal, despite having had *half* the components taken out of it. These dishes have been created with *you* in mind, so you can cook delicious food everyone can enjoy, with confidence and in the comfort of your own home.

Vegan or not, we hope this book will encourage everyone to explore the joy of food. When we first went vegan, we seized the opportunity to break away from our old faithful Western and Italian dishes, which were heavy in meat and dairy, and instead threw ourselves into Asian cuisine. This was easy to veganise and distanced us from our previous cooking habits. As time went on however, we re-introduced those pre-loved classics back into our repertoire in their new vegan forms. We found we still enjoyed them just as much now, if not more! People often worry they are going to 'miss out', or not be able to enjoy all their old favourites but there is almost always a way to reinvent or replicate a dish.

Think of it as a new beginning for your health – and for your taste buds too.

We still live on the road and our kitchen is still tiny. We are minimalists in the extreme and we don't even own a whisk, although we have added a benchtop oven to our scant range of equipment. Almost every kitchen item you see in this book has been either gifted, borrowed or bought from charity shops. We reduce, reuse, recycle and live a no-waste lifestyle, consuming only what we need. We still haven't managed to fit into the stereotype of being 'skinny, unhealthy vegans', yet.

But these days, my mum tells people: 'Talk to my daughter about going vegan. She eats really well'.

EVERYDAY

Our Vegan Pantry

When learning any new way of cooking or eating, the last thing anyone wants is for that transition to be hard, or expensive. When adapting to a vegan lifestyle, at first it may feel as though you are paying out a huge amount for all kinds of new and strange foods, but don't be too alarmed. When you cook vegan from scratch, the majority of ingredients are nothing out of the ordinary; we just use more beans, herbs and spices. Most of the items listed here have been right there in your local supermarket the whole time. The occasion may have just never arisen to buy them before! Once you have them in your kitchen, you are well set up to make all kind of vegan dishes easily and often cheaply, as a little goes a long way.

The food items listed below are mentioned regularly throughout this book. They are all good staples to keep in your pantry and should be available from most supermarkets, vegan or gluten-free shops, and/or from Asian grocers. We have kept things pretty basic, as when we went vegan, this was all we had access to and even now, is still all we really need and use. There are a multitude of other fantastic products out there and it is always fun to try out new foods and experiment. There are also many other items other vegans would no doubt list as their 'basics', too. When it comes to making the recipes in this book however, this is pretty much all you'll require, to go hand-in-hand with your everyday fruit and vegetables.

Herbs and Spices

Herbs and spices are a vegan cook's best friend. Our pantry contains more of these than anything else. If you've never really used them much before, you'll wonder what you ever did without them! These are the ones we use most often, either fresh, dried or in paste form:

Our Vegan Pantry

Dried Herbs

basil

bay leaves

cayenne pepper

chilli flakes

chilli paste (this comes in a jar or tube. Just make sure you check the label first to make sure there are no milk products listed, some do)

chilli powder

Chinese five spice

cinnamon

coriander (most commonly ground coriander, but also coriander seeds. Be wary of fresh coriander (a.k.a. cilantro) or the seeds in tubes or jars, as again these can contain milk)

cumin (most commonly ground cumin, but also cumin seeds)

curry paste (again, check the label before purchasing, as some curry pastes, particularly red or green curries can contain shrimp)

curry powder

garam masala

ginger (fresh ginger root, or you can use ready-made, crushed ginger)

garlic (fresh, but garlic powder is also frequently used in vegan recipes)

ground cloves

kala namak (a.k.a. black salt, for imparting an 'eggy' or 'umami' taste to dishes)

mixed herbs

mustard (most commonly Dijon, however whole seed and hot mustard is also handy)

onion powder oregano

paprika

rosemary

sage

sesame seeds (most commonly white, but you can also use black or unhulled)

smoked paprika

sriracha (This is very popular in vegan cooking. However, if you wish to avoid onion or garlic we suggest using plain hot sauce or chilli paste in place of this.)

sweet chilli sauce (As above, this is also very popular, however it does contain garlic too, so if cooking for intolerances we suggest that you don't use it.)

thyme

turmeric

wasabi (we use the ready-made paste in a tube)

PLEASE NOTE: When quoted in the recipes, herbs are presumed to be dried unless specifically stated otherwise.

Fresh Herbs

Basil, coriander (cilantro), parsley, rosemary and thyme are the fresh herbs we use most regularly. If you have the room, we definitely recommend growing your own, as it can really keep the cost down - not to mention that once you start using them, you are going to want to put them in everything!

Other Everyday Staples

Almond milk - this dairy-free milk is available from the long-life milk section of the supermarket and is always useful to have on hand.

Beans - specifically kidney beans, black beans and cannellini beans. There are plenty more such as pinto and butter beans but the first three are the ones you will find in this book. Don't panic if you find yourself without one of them, however. They are all very interchangeable and forgiving. Canned or dried, the preference is yours. Many people prefer to buy them dried and do the soaking and cooking themselves. For the record though, we're lazy and use tinned.

Chickpeas - also known as garbanzo beans. These delightfully nutty little golden nuggets are the main ingredient in such delectable delights as Hummus and all sorts of other Middle-Eastern and Mediterranean dishes. Like beans, they are cheap to buy both tinned or dried and are a good source of protein, carbohydrate and fibre. This makes them suitable for throwing in many soups, stews or salads. You can also simply roast them in the oven, either plain or sprinkled with chilli, garlic powder or cumin to make a crunchy snack or salad topper.

Our Vegan Pantry

Coconut milk or coconut cream is our usual go-to for making creamy soups, curries and sauces. Mega-useful and versatile, we always grab a tin or two when shopping. Many people have a preference when it comes to using full fat or lite and you are welcome to use the lower-fat version, however we use regular for our recipes, as the difference in flavour and texture is quite marked.

Dangmyeon – also known as 'glass noodles'. These Korean noodles are gluten-free and made from sweet potato starch. We love to use these in gluten-free dishes as they are more substantial than other gluten-free noodles, such as mung bean vermicelli, and they hold their shape much better than rice noodles.

Dried mushrooms are brilliant for using in stocks, soups, stir fries – anywhere you would normally use fresh mushrooms. While their flavour is rich, they are an affordable luxury and will enhance any dish you use them in. Before using them in cooking, it is best to rehydrate them first in hot water. This plumps up the mushrooms and makes them more pleasant for eating. As a bonus, the water you soak them in also creates a flavourful broth, which you can use in recipes just as you would regular stock. The most common varieties include shiitake, porcini, oyster and chanterelles. We like to have a selection as they are all delicious! Once opened, keep your dried mushrooms in a sealed Ziplock bag or container, in a dark place. You can also keep them in the freezer.

Edamame – are fresh, green soybeans and are available from the freezer aisle of your supermarket. They come whole in pods or ready-shelled for convenience. They are quick to cook much like peas and are delicious hot or cold. Great for salads, 'dragon bowls' and a wide range of Asian-style dishes.

Flax seed is found in supermarket health food aisles. Flax seed (a.k.a. linseed) has been grown since the beginning of civilisation and it is loaded with nutrients. fresh tasting, with a subtle, nutty flavour, you can sprinkle it on all kinds of things such as salads, cereal or in smoothies and dairy-free yoghurt. It's also the one of the easiest and most common 'binders' to use in place of egg in vegan cooking, when mixed with water.

Lemon juice or lime juice is something where good quality really counts. If you can't access or afford fresh lemons or limes, at least aim to pay a little more for really good quality bottled juice. It lasts for ages and your dishes will taste so much better.

Lentils. Yes, vegans really do eat lentils, lots of them. red, brown, black, yellow and even green. Canned or dried, take your pick. They are equally versatile and

Our Vegan Pantry

interchangeable, but you will only see red and brown in this book, as they are the most commonly available. Red lentils are the preferred dried option, as they are quick to cook and are very helpful when it comes to thickening and adding texture to things such as soups, stews and curries. Brown lentils are just as delicious in all of those, but, being a little larger and plumper they hold their form better, making them suitable for salads, burgers and more.

Mayonnaise – vegan, of course! There are some excellent ones. Use them just as you do regular mayo, or jazz them up with some of our quick suggestions in the 'Sauces, Dressings and Gravies' chapter.

Miso. This yummy paste made from fermented soybeans has been a plant-based protein source in Japanese cooking for hundreds of years. Miso paste imparts a delicious flavour to stocks, soups and many other vegan dishes.

Nuts. Before we went vegan, nuts were something we only used to have at Christmas. Don't be like us, you deserve so much better! Nuts are such a delicious and nutritious addition to so many things. almonds, Brazils, cashews, peanuts, pine nuts, walnuts – you get the idea. Start sprinkling a few on your cereal or salads and see how much better they taste.

Nutritional yeast is not to be confused with brewer's or baking yeast. Nutritional yeast is a seasoning used to impart a 'cheesy' flavour to vegan sauces, soups and other dishes. Commonly abbreviated to 'nooch', you can find it in the health food aisle at supermarkets. Despite it looking rather like sawdust, it is full of vitamins and minerals and those who love the savoury taste like to sprinkle it on absolutely everything.

Olive oil. We try and use as little oil as possible in our cooking, however when we do need to add it, olive oil is the one we keep on hand. We like its versatility and flavour and find it to be the friendliest to those with allergies and food sensitivities.

Peanut butter is used for so much more than spreading on toast in vegan cooking, such as sauces, dressings and stir fries.

Pickled jalapeños. We always keep a jar of these on hand for recipes and everyday uses such as salads, sandwiches and lunch wraps. You can of course use fresh chilli peppers, and we use those too, but having these in the fridge or pantry means we never get caught out not being able to get fresh ones. They are so quick and convenient any time you want to add a little zing.

Polenta is not a vegan staple. However, we have used it in this book in several recipes rather than using gluten-containing flours. You'll find it in the baking section of your supermarket.

Quinoa (pronounced 'keen-wah') is one of those annoyingly trendy uber-foods. It's an ancient, South American, gluten-free seed that can be used in place of rice or pasta, both as an ingredient or as an accompaniment to many dishes. It's just as easy to cook as rice or pasta too. Don't let the weird spelling put you off.

Refried beans. These cooked and mashed beans are a staple in Mexican and Latin American cooking and can be plain or spicy. They are most often used to make dips or nachos, however their firm texture makes them ideal for putting on pizzas, stuffing courgettes and making burgers. Just be sure to check the ingredients before purchasing, as some brands still use the Mexican tradition of including lard (pig fat) in their refried beans.

Rice Vinegar. Also known as rice wine vinegar, this Asian ingredient is one and the same and can be readily bought in the international section of supermarkets.

Seeds – chia, pumpkin, sesame, sunflower – the list goes on. Like all-natural whole foods, they are all good for you and the only limit is your imagination. Sprinkle them on salads and cereals, in smoothies and over dishes for an extra subtle and nutritious boost.

Sesame oil isn't an oil normally used for general cooking in recipes unless specified. However, it is delicious used in small amounts when making Asian dips, salad dressings and stir fries.

Soy milk, as with almond milk, or other commonly used non-dairy milks, is available from the long-life milk section of the supermarket. It has a plainer, less nutty flavour than almond milk and is always useful to keep in the pantry.

Stocks

You will see that beef-style, chicken-style or vegetable stock is referred to a lot in this book. Brands such as Massel, or Vegeta are readily available in the supermarket. They contain no animal products and have the added bonus of being gluten-free and even low FODMAP. They are most commonly found in stock cubes, or powder form, but also come in ready-made liquid cartons.

Make Your Own Vegetable Stock

As you might imagine, vegans get through a heap of fresh produce and you can make a handy saving on constantly buying vegetable stock by making your own from all your discarded peelings, stalks and odds and ends. You can't beat the flavour and quality of home-made and it's so easy. We keep a stock bag in the freezer and add to it throughout the week as we prepare our meals. Some things you can put in it include Onion (tops, bottoms and skins), Mushrooms, Celery Leaves and Stalks, Garlic (skins and all), Carrots (all parts), Potatoes (all parts) as well as many other scraps and peelings such as Pumpkin, Capsicums and fresh herbs. The only ones we tend to leave out are Broccoli, Cauliflower and Cabbage, as they can make your stock taste a little bitter.

When your stock bag is full, put everything into a large pot and fill it with water until all the scraps are covered. Bring to the boil, then reduce the heat to low and simmer for at least 30 minutes (I like to allow an hour). Once cool, strain your stock and dispose of the vegetable scraps in your compost bin or refuse. Transfer your lovely home-made stock to Ziplock bags or airtight containers, where it will keep in the fridge for four days, or in the freezer for up to three months.

Tahini is made from sesame seeds and found in the nut butters section of supermarkets. Tahini is a nutritious and versatile addition to any vegan kitchen. In its plainest form you can spread it on toast, instead of butter, but you can also use it to make Falafel, dips or our favourite, dressings.

Tamari is similar to soy sauce and is used exactly the same way in cooking. Any time you see tamari in our recipes, you are welcome to use light (Japanese-style) soy sauce instead, or if you prefer, the heavier Chinese-style soy sauce. However, we prefer to use tamari over soy as it is gluten-free, whereas regular soy sauce is usually made with wheat. Like soy sauce, you can also buy low-sodium versions of Tamari if you are conscious of reducing salt intake.

Tinned Tomatoes. Of course, you can always use fresh tomatoes in place of tinned if you have them, but we always keep at least a couple of tins on hand. They are useful when it comes to making so many recipes, from soups to mains.

Tofu. Also known as bean curd, tofu is of course one of the most well-known vegan foods, although that doesn't mean all vegans eat it. Many do however, because aside from being a handy source of protein, it can be cooked in all sorts of ways and can take the form of many flavours. It comes in several varieties, such as silken, soft or firm, however the one we use is almost always firm or extra firm.

NB: You won't find other alternatives such as Tempeh or Seitan in this book, as it was more than two years before we were able to find any. For those of you who can though, and would like to cook with it, head straight to Google, or better still, a vegan friend who has been there and done that.

Our Vegan Pantry

How to Drain and Press Tofu

You'll see in our recipes that we always recommend you 'drain and press' your tofu before cooking. Most packaged tofu has a high moisture content that requires draining before using. This is so your tofu will hold its shape and absorb more flavours while cooking or marinating. Opening the packet and draining the contents will remove some of the liquid but 'pressing' is usually required to remove the rest of the liquid.

There are various ways people like to do this, but in our kitchen, we do it by sandwiching the tofu between a chopping board and another flat object, such as a plate. Using our body weight, we press down on the plate or object, squeezing the moisture out of the tofu but being careful not to crush it and ruin its structure. We do this until liquid is no longer noticeably coming out of the tofu.

Exactly how much moisture we try and remove depends on what the tofu is going to be used for. If it is going to be marinating, such as when making Tofu Bacon (page 40), the less moisture there is to start with, the more marinade it will absorb, which is what you want. If simply coating and frying, such as when making Crispy Tofu (page 98) you need not worry too much, as the moisture helps the coating stick. When making burgers, such as the Almost Egg Burger (page 85) which requires you to cut slabs, it can be easier to drain the excess moisture, cut the tofu into slabs, and then place the slabs on a clean tea towel or paper towels, so they can drain further without being damaged in the pressing. Don't worry if this all sounds like a lot of fluffing around, you'll soon be doing it like a pro!

Worcestershire sauce (pronounced 'wooster sauce') is not used as frequently as tamari or soy but is still a good item to keep on hand. However, be sure to check the label before purchasing. While there are vegan-friendly brands available, some do contain anchovy.

Breakfasts

One of the questions people most often ask about vegan food is, 'What do you eat for breakfast?'

The first meal of the day is actually one of the easiest, as many traditional breakfast options are actually the same, or very similar, as for non-vegans. Last time we checked, apples were still vegan, as are bananas and all the other fruits people routinely grab when they're heading out the door in the morning. You can still have toast, with dairy-free spread and Marmite, Promite, Vegemite, peanut butter, jam or conserve of your choice. Many vegans can serve up avocado on toast as well as any cafe, with sweet cherry tomatoes, a sprinkle of lemon juice or black pepper, or red chilli flakes. You can still have many cereals, with dairy-free milk. You can make delicious and nutritious smoothies, using fresh fruit, vegetables and plant-based milk alternatives like almond milk or oat milk. And, you *can* still enjoy a hearty fry-up with all the works, to set you up for the day. Here are some of our favourite traditional, and not-so-traditional ideas for a delicious vegan breakfast.

Best Breakfast Mushrooms

WHEAT/GLUTEN FREE　GRAIN FREE　ALLIUM FREE

We know what you're thinking. 'Mushrooms are just mushrooms.' Right? Just chuck them in a pan and move them around a bit and that's all there is to it. Pretty much. But there is a secret to cooking the perfect breakfast mushrooms, and once you try these, you'll never go back. You can jazz them up by adding fresh parsley, garlic or lemon but this is the basic, never-fail formula. You're welcome!

Serves 2

Ingredients:

200 g whole button mushrooms, wiped (just wipe them over with a slightly damp paper towel to remove any traces of dirt)

2 tbsp olive oil

¼ tsp salt, or more, to taste

freshly ground black pepper

Method:

Heat a large frying pan over medium heat. When warm, add the olive oil.

Add the mushrooms to the pan, spreading them out in a single layer. Cook, *without moving them* for 3 to 5 minutes. Gently turn them over, then cook another 3 to 5 minutes, or until golden brown on all sides. While still in the pan, season with a generous scrunch of salt and pepper

Remove from the pan and enjoy on their own, on toast, or as part of a delicious 'big breaky' fry-up.

Breakfast Salad

WHEAT/GLUTEN FREE | GRAIN FREE | ALLIUM FREE

If you had told me years ago that salad would be my favourite choice for breakfast, I would never have believed it. But why eat boring toast or cereal for breakfast when you can start your day with a rainbow? A lot of people think it's weird – but don't knock it until you try it. It's amazing how long a simple salad will sustain you; it's unlike any other breakfast I've ever tried and still keeps me going well after lunchtime. You can add whatever you like, but this is my basic everyday formula. It's a fresh, energising and super healthy way to kick the day off. I love it with leftover Tofu Bacon (page 40) crumbled over the top too!

Serves 1

Ingredients:

large handful baby spinach leaves (or whatever salad leaves you like)

3 – 4 cherry tomatoes, halved

2-inch chunk cucumber, roughly chopped

½ avocado, peeled and chopped

1 tbsp tahini

handful mung bean sprouts

1 tbsp fresh herbs (I use either coriander or basil, finely chopped – optional but delicious)

1 tbsp sunflower seeds

1 tbsp pumpkin seeds

tamari for dressing (or you can also use balsamic vinegar or whatever else you might like)

Method:

In a small to medium bowl (a regular cereal bowl will do), put in your spinach or salad leaves.

Add the chopped tomato, cucumber and avocado on top of the spinach. Dollop the tahini on top of those.

Pile up the mung beans on top of the salad, followed by the fresh herbs if you decide to use them. Sprinkle the sunflower and pumpkin seeds on top and finish with a generous splash of tamari, or your favourite dressing.

Breakfasts

French Hot Chocolate Bowls with Buttery Baguettes

Being vegan doesn't mean being restricted to the same old toast, oatmeal and smoothies. Everyone loves to indulge themselves sometimes and this is the ultimate vegan luxury breakfast. One of Gareth's favourite childhood memories is visiting family in France and slurping on steaming bowls of hot, molten chocolate as a treat. 'Something to put fat in my cheeks for the grandparents to squeeze!' Just the thing for frosty mornings and freezing winter days, or those times when you just feel like being a couch potato. What better way to coddle yourself, or pamper loved ones, than with a big, comforting bowl of silky-smooth, dark chocolate, coupled with a stack of soft, buttery dunkers?

Makes 2 small bowls or one BIG bowl.

Ingredients:

75g dark chocolate (we use 70% dark chocolate), chopped into very small pieces

3 cups almond or other dairy-free milk

1 small baguette, cut into slices and 'buttered' with dairy-free spread (or you can use toast, cut into triangles)

Dairy-free spread

Method:

Put the almond milk into a medium-sized saucepan over medium heat. While the milk is warming up, break up the chocolate into pieces and chop it as finely as you can (this helps the chocolate melt faster and gives a smoother result). Add the chocolate to the milk and stir well. Bring to the boil, then reduce the heat to low, stirring all the time until the chocolate is completely melted.

Remove from the heat and carefully pour, or ladle, into bowls. Cut your baguette into slices and spread each one with dairy-free spread.

Serve, with much joyful slurping and dunking.

Breakfasts

Hash—o—Bello Burger

CAN BE MADE BOTH

WHEAT/GLUTEN FREE ALLIUM FREE

One of Gareth's special creations, it should perhaps be called the 'Hangover Burger', as that is when it really hits the spot, but it's far too delicious to save just for those 'off days'. This is about as close as we get to junk food and while it may not be the healthiest breakfast, some days you just don't care. Drizzle with lashings of your favourite sauce and enjoy with gusto. If you prefer to use less oil, you can bake your hash browns rather than pan frying. Amounts here are for one delectable burger, but you can of course multiply the ingredients to make more.

Serves 1

Ingredients:

1 burger bun per person (our favourite is ciabatta)

1 hash brown per person (note: not all frozen hash browns are vegan, some contain milk products so check the ingredients first)

olive oil, for frying

1 large portobello mushroom per burger

dairy-free butter, for spreading the buns (or you can use hummus)

favourite burger toppings of choice: e.g. lettuce, tomato, vegan mayo or sweet chilli sauce (omit the sweet chilli sauce if you are intolerant to garlic or onion)

Method:

First, either bake or fry your hash browns according to package directions, then set aside to keep warm.

Heat a little oil in a bottom of a frying pan over medium heat and add in your mushroom(s). Cook gently for 5 to 8 minutes on each side, turning over at least once until tender. Remove from the pan and place on a plate lined with paper towel, to drain any excess oil.

Slice the burger buns in half. You may like to crisp them up a little in the pan first, or you can simply have them fresh. Now to build the burgers! Spread the buns with dairy-free butter or hummus, then add your lettuce and/or other salad garnishes.

Next, stack your hash brown and mushroom, then drizzle with sweet chilli or other sauce, place the top half of the bun on your burger and serve.

Breakfasts

Real Proper Tofu Scramble

WHEAT/GLUTEN FREE   GRAIN FREE   ALLIUM FREE

Tofu is a wonderfully versatile source of protein, which is also able to wear the guise of many foods. This recipe makes it look and taste uncannily like authentic scrambled egg! The secret is kala namak – or black salt. Its pungent, sulphurous smell imparts a perfect eggy flavour. If you can't find black salt in your supermarket, you can find it in Asian grocery stores. A less firm tofu is best for this recipe, as you want it to go nice and crumbly, like the traditional scramble. We recommend using soy milk, or another 'plain' tasting plant milk if possible, as it gives a more authentic flavour. Once cooked, enjoy just as you would regular scrambled egg, on toast or as part of a full breakfast. For those who like a little heat, we can highly recommend a squeeze of hot sauce!

Serves 3

39

Ingredients:

1 pack firm tofu, drained and pressed

2 tbsp nutritional yeast

½ tsp turmeric

½ tsp paprika

¼ tsp black salt

1 tsp Dijon mustard

1 tbsp dairy-free butter

1/3 cup soy, or other dairy-free milk

Scrunch of regular salt, and freshly ground black pepper, to taste

Method:

Put the drained and pressed tofu into a large bowl and mash well with a fork. You want it to be nice and crumbly but not too fine. Add the nutritional yeast, turmeric, paprika, black salt, Dijon mustard and soy milk to the bowl of crumbled tofu and mix all together, gently but thoroughly, until everything is well combined.

In a large saucepan, heat the dairy-free butter over medium-high heat until it has melted. Add in the tofu mixture and cook for around 8 minutes, moving it around the pan as it cooks, until it is well heated through and golden on all sides. Taste for seasoning, adding a scrunch of regular salt and pepper as desired. Remove from the pan and serve.

Breakfasts

Tofu 'Bacon'

CAN BE MADE

OIL FREE WHEAT/GLUTEN FREE ALLIUM FREE

This recipe is ridiculously easy and makes a huge number of delicious 'rashers', for a fraction of the price of the real thing. However, while the marinade is quick to make, the tofu is best left to marinade overnight - or at least four hours, to maximise the flavour. Give it a go and we're sure you'll agree; this recipe really delivers.

Serves 4, or more

Ingredients:

1 block of extra firm tofu, drained and pressed (the firmer you can get, the better)

oil for frying (optional, you can choose to fry without oil)

For the marinade:

1 cup water

2 tbsp Worcestershire sauce (check the ingredients to make sure its vegan, some contain fish)

¾ cup tamari

2 tbsp maple syrup

2 tbsp tomato paste

1 tbsp smoked paprika

Method:

First, drain and press the tofu. Take care not to press the block too hard; you don't want it to crumble or lose its shape. Using a sharp knife, slice the block long ways into thin strips. The broader the knife, the easier it is to cut into nice, thin slices.

To make the marinade, you need a litre size container (or bigger) with a lid. Put in the water, Worcestershire sauce and tamari first, followed by the maple syrup, tomato paste and smoked paprika. Mix all together well, then pop in your sliced tofu, keeping it well covered with the marinade. Set aside for at least four hours, or even overnight. When ready to use, remove the tofu rashers and shake off excess liquid. Heat a frying pan on medium-high heat, adding a little oil if desired. Add the tofu slices to the pan one at a time, frying for a few minutes on each side and turning regularly, until browned and crisp. Remove from the pan and place on a plate, lined with paper towel to remove excess oil. Serve as desired, just as you would regular bacon. Leftovers are delicious hot or cold, crumbled into a salad!

Breakfasts

Soups

I've been a soup fanatic as long as I can remember. I make them so often, we could have filled a whole book with soup recipes alone. Making magical vegan soup is easy when so many recipes already are. A delicious batch of soupy goodness can keep a person well fed for several meals, often at next to no cost. Best of all, you can make it according to however you're feeling. To me, soup is love in a ladle. It can be light and healthy, or warm and comforting; whatever you need it to be. Whether you're after something soothing and nourishing when you're ill, or something plain cheap and tasty for when you're broke, there is always a soup to suit. This chapter has them all.

Easy Vegan Pho

OIL FREE WHEAT/GLUTEN FREE ALLIUM FREE

Vietnamese Pho is one of my favourite soups but was one I bought ready-made for a long time, as making my own seemed much too hard. All the recipes I came across sounded so hard and were full of random, exotic ingredients the average person couldn't lay hands on. Eventually I had enough and decided to develop my own version, using every day, easily sourced ingredients. It may not be authentic, but is nice and simple and hits the spot, with its delicately spiced broth and flavoursome garnishes. The more you load it up, the taster it gets!

Serves 4 - 6

Ingredients:

3 litres vegetable stock

2" piece fresh ginger, peeled and cut in half

¼ tsp ground cloves

½ tsp cinnamon

¾ tsp ground coriander

1 block of firm tofu, drained, pressed and cut into cubes

3 cups chopped vegetables - e.g. broccoli, bok choy, mushrooms, spinach

50g rice or sweet potato noodles

2 tbsp tamari (or more, as desired)

Lime juice

Mung bean sprouts and fresh, chopped coriander, to garnish

Method:

Put the vegetable stock into a large soup pan over medium heat, along with the ginger, ground cloves, cinnamon and ground coriander. Bring to the boil, reduce the heat to low and simmer for 20 minutes. Remove the pieces of ginger and discard.

Add the tofu to the pan, along with the chopped vegetables. Simmer for another 5 minutes, then add the noodles and cook until done, according to packet directions.

Serve, adding tamari and lime juice to taste. Top with bean sprouts and fresh coriander (cilantro). You can also add sriracha if you want more spice.

Soups

Hot and Sour Soup

CAN BE MADE

OIL FREE	WHEAT/GLUTEN FREE	GRAIN FREE

The first time I tried hot and sour soup was years ago in Bali. I loved it, but once I was back home, I failed to find any version which came close to tasting like the 'real deal'. Eventually I just came up with my own recipe and at last my taste buds were happily satisfied. This delicious vegan version is very healthy but also very spicy, so if you don't like the flavour too hot, I would recommend reducing the amount of chilli paste. You can also make it oil-free by simply omitting the oil and cooking the garlic and ginger in a quarter-cup of water instead, I just like the flavour the peanut oil gives.

Serves 4

Ingredients:

1 tbsp peanut oil (optional)

1 tbsp fresh ginger, peeled and finely chopped

5 cloves garlic, finely chopped or crushed

2 litres vegetable stock (we recommend using either home-made or the ready-made, store-bought liquid stocks for the best results)

200g mushrooms, sliced, stalks on

1 small can bamboo shoots, drained

1 medium-sized bunch bok choy (or other Asian greens of choice), sliced

2 tbsp rice vinegar

1 tbsp red chilli paste, or to taste

2 tbsp tamari

1 tbsp brown sugar

3 spring onions, sliced

¼ cup fresh coriander (cilantro), finely chopped

fresh mung bean sprouts, for garnish

Method:

Heat the peanut oil (or water, if omitting the oil) in a large saucepan over medium heat. Add the ginger and garlic and fry for a minute, stirring so as not to let it burn. Pour in the vegetable stock and bring it to the boil.

Reduce the heat, then add in the sliced mushrooms and bamboo shoots. Simmer gently for 15 minutes. Throw in the bok choy, along with the rice vinegar, chilli paste, tamari and brown sugar and stir well, then simmer for another 10 – 15 minutes. At this stage, you can test your soup for seasoning and add more chilli paste if you would like more 'zing'. Stir in the sliced spring onions and coriander and serve, topped with the mung bean sprouts.

Lentil & Rosemary Soup

OIL FREE   WHEAT/GLUTEN FREE   ALLIUM FREE

This is a real 'hug in a bowl' for those days when you want something hearty and comforting, without too much hassle. Chunky and delicious, it's bursting with flavour. The great thing about not cooking with onion and garlic is that it makes preparation so much faster, too! You are welcome to add it in if you wish, however it's the fresh rosemary which is the star here. The flavour intensifies over time, making it a perfect lunch option to enjoy through the working week!

Serves 4

Ingredients:

¼ cup water

2 stalks celery, chopped

1 large carrot, or 2 small, peeled and diced

1 x 400g can chopped tomatoes

4 cups vegetable stock

1 x 400g can brown lentils, rinsed well and drained

½ cup red lentils

½ tsp fresh rosemary (or more, to taste) finely chopped

salt and freshly ground black pepper

Method:

Put the ¼ cup of water into a large saucepan on medium-high heat. Add in the carrot and celery and sauté for five minutes, stirring occasionally. Add in the tomatoes, stock, brown and red lentils and the finely chopped rosemary and mix together well. Bring to the boil, then reduce the heat and simmer for 25 minutes, until both the lentils and vegetables are tender.

Taste for seasoning, and add salt and pepper as required.

Delicious served with a chunk of warm, crusty bread and dairy-free butter!

Soups

Man 'Flu Minestrone

I came up with this recipe a couple of years ago, when Gareth came down with the 'flu. There's no worse 'flu in existence than 'Man 'Flu', as most of us know, and I wanted to make him something really hearty and comforting to help him feel better. This rich, chunky soup definitely did the trick and these days it's the first resort whenever the dreaded bugs are looming. Make sure you include the fresh basil, if you have it. It really adds to the flavour but not only that, basil is a natural anti-inflammatory – nature's own form of aspirin. *Let food be thy medicine.*

Makes 4 man-sized servings, or 6 regular!

Ingredients:

¼ cup water

1 onion, finely chopped

3 cloves garlic, finely chopped or crushed

2 – 3 celery sticks, diced

2 carrots, peeled and diced

2 x 400g cans chopped tomatoes

3 cups water

1 x 400g can cannellini beans, rinsed well and drained (or use kidney beans)

1 cup or small can peas or green beans, rinsed and drained (or frozen)

3 tbsp tomato paste

1 cup small pasta, such as shells or macaroni (use gluten-free pasta if required)

1 cup fresh spinach or silver beet

½ tsp oregano

¼ tsp thyme

¼ cup fresh basil, chopped salt and freshly ground black pepper, to taste

Method:

Heat the first quarter-cup of water in a large saucepan over medium heat. Add the onion and garlic and cook for a few minutes until the onion has softened. Add the celery, carrots and tinned tomatoes and bring to the boil. Reduce the heat and simmer gently for five minutes.

Add in the rest of the water, followed by the cannellini beans, green beans or peas, tomato paste, pasta, spinach and dried herbs. Mix well and bring back up to the boil, then lower the heat again and let bubble away for 25 – 30 minutes, until the vegetables and pasta are tender. Stir in the chopped, fresh basil and season to taste with salt and pepper.

Serve yummy, steaming hot bowl of goodness to patient (and have one for yourself, too)!

Soups

Mapo Tofu Soup

WHEAT/GLUTEN FREE GRAIN FREE ALLIUM FREE

This recipe is an accidental twist on the traditional Chinese mapo tofu dish. I was making it one night for dinner and hadn't got around to thickening it when Gareth sidled up for a sneaky taste. Upon sampling the broth, he exclaimed, 'Ooh, I like this soup!' 'It's not ready yet!' I berated him, but after tasting it myself (and with him begging me to leave it as it was), I had to agree, it did indeed make a darn good soup. Spicy and pungent, it's requested often in our household. I use five spice in place of the traditional Szechuan peppercorns – and everyone always loves the flavour.

Serves 4

Ingredients:

1 large handful dried mushrooms, pre-soaked in water for 30 minutes

1 packet firm tofu, drained and pressed

1 ½ tbsp peanut oil

half-inch piece fresh ginger, peeled and finely chopped or crushed

3 – 4 button mushrooms, sliced

3 cups water

1 vegetable stock cube

2 tbsp tamari

2 tbsp sesame oil

2 tbsp miso paste

1 tbsp chilli paste

1 tsp five spice

salt and freshly ground black pepper, to taste

Method:

First, put the dried mushrooms into a bowl and cover them with hot water. Set aside and leave them to soak for 30 minutes, until slightly softened. While they are rehydrating you can get started on making the rest of the soup. Cut the drained, pressed tofu into half-inch cubes. In a large pan, heat the peanut oil over medium heat. Add the ginger and sliced fresh mushrooms and sauté for a couple of minutes. Add the tofu to the pan, followed by the water, stock cube, tamari, sesame oil, miso, chilli paste and five spice. Bring to the boil, then add the dried mushrooms. You can add a little of the mushroom-y liquid from the bowl they've been soaking in, to give a little richness to the flavour. Reduce the heat to low and simmer for 5 – 10 minutes. Season to taste with freshly ground black pepper. Only add salt if necessary and be sure not to do so without tasting first, as you may well find the broth is already rich enough. Serve and enjoy!

Mexican Black Bean Soup

CAN BE MADE

OIL FREE · WHEAT/GLUTEN FREE · ALLIUM FREE

Imagine a delicious bean burrito filling as a bowl of stupendous soup! This recipe makes a big pot, bursting with colour and flavour. Perfect for chilly days, or when you need a little comfort food.

Serves 4

Ingredients:

¼ cup water

1 large onion, finely chopped (optional, can be omitted)

3 cloves garlic, finely chopped or crushed (optional, can be omitted)

2 carrots, peeled and diced

1 whole red capsicum, diced

1 x 400g tin chopped tomatoes

1 x 400g tin whole kernel corn

2 X 400g cans black beans, drained and rinsed

1 jalapeño, deseeded and finely diced

3 cups vegetable stock

4 tbsp lime juice

1 - 2 tsp ground cumin

1 - 2 tsp ground coriander

1 - 2 tsp paprika

½ - 1 tsp chilli powder (or less, to taste)

Salt and pepper

½ an avocado, cut into slices and fresh coriander (cilantro) (optional) to garnish

Method:

Heat the water in a large pot over medium heat. Sauté the onion and garlic until softened, then add the carrot and capsicum and cook another five minutes. Add the tomatoes, corn, beans, jalapeño, vegetable stock and lime juice.

Next, add one teaspoon each of the ground cumin, coriander and paprika and half a teaspoon of the chilli powder. Mix well, then bring to the boil and simmer gently for 30 minutes, adding more water if necessary. You want it to look soupy, not a burrito filling!

Taste the sauce for seasoning and add the rest of the spices to taste if needed, along with salt and pepper. Serve with crusty bread, or corn chips, garnished with a few slices of avocado and fresh coriander (cilantro).

Soups

My Miso Soup

OIL FREE   WHEAT/GLUTEN FREE   ALLIUM FREE

When I feel like miso soup, I want it fast, without too much mucking about. This version is far from authentic but is nonetheless my favourite and has been developed after trying many, many different ones. It's cheap, light and healthy and is quick to throw together. I often make this in the mornings and just put everything in the pan, then go about my usual routine while it simmers away, until it's time to add the noodles. It's also my go-to for work lunches during the week and like all the best soups, the flavour improves and intensifies with time. This is my basic recipe, which uses dangmyeon – sweet potato noodles, to make it gluten-free but you can substitute these with whatever noodles you like. You can adapt it to include finely chopped spring onion, cubed tofu, or any other favourite additions.

Serves 2

Ingredients:

5 cups water

1 vegan chicken style stock cube

2 tbsp tamari

2 tbsp miso paste

large handful dried mushrooms
(or you can use fresh, sliced)

50g noodles

Handful baby spinach leaves

2 tbsp fresh coriander (cilantro), chopped, plus extra for garnish
fresh lemon or lime juice, to taste

Method:

Put the five cups of water in a large pan over medium-high heat. Add the stock cube, tamari, miso paste and mushrooms and stir. Bring to the boil, reduce the heat and simmer for 20 minutes, stirring occasionally to make sure the dried mushrooms get covered with the broth. After 20 minutes, add in the noodles and simmer another 10 minutes, until tender. Add more water if needed, as the noodles and dried mushrooms can absorb some of the liquid. Add the baby spinach and fresh coriander and stir through, then taste for seasoning, adding fresh lemon or lime juice to reach the desired flavour. Serve, garnished with extra coriander.

Soups

Rainy Day Vegetable Soup

OIL FREE   WHEAT/GLUTEN FREE   ALLIUM FREE

Of course, you don't have to save this soup just for rainy days. But that's always when I feel compelled to make it and it's one of those soups which just makes your day better and fills you with lots of healthy veggies, as well as warm fuzzies. . Quick to cook, with minimum fuss, it's ideal to throw together on busy family weekends, or for several work lunches. You can of course adapt it to include any other sad looking bits and pieces you have lurking in the fridge, such as broccoli, cabbage, whatever you have. It's pretty much impossible to get wrong!

Serves 4

Ingredients:

¼ cup water

2 carrots, peeled and diced

2 stalks celery, diced

1 medium potato, peeled and cut into large dices

4 cups vegetable stock

1 x 400g can chopped tomatoes

1 x 400g can kidney beans, rinsed well and drained

1 small can sweetcorn, drained (or you can use frozen)

1 small can peas, drained (again, you can also use frozen)

1 tsp oregano

large pinch chilli flakes

salt and freshly ground black pepper, to taste

fresh parsley (optional, to garnish)

Method:

Put the quarter-cup of water into a large pan on medium heat. Add the carrots and celery along with a good scrunch of salt and pepper and sauté for 5 minutes, stirring regularly and adding more water if the vegetables are getting too dry. Add the diced potato, followed by the stock, tomatoes, beans, sweetcorn, peas, oregano and chilli flakes. Bring to the boil, reduce the heat and simmer gently for 30 minutes, or until the vegetables are tender.

Taste for seasoning, adding salt and pepper as desired, then serve.

Soups

Suzy's Farmhouse Pumpkin Soup

I came up with this recipe one weekend when we were house-sitting in a beautiful old farmhouse with a huge kitchen and a coal range. It was raining and I felt like making soup but without my own ingredients on hand I had to wing it and make it up as I went along, using whatever I could find. The result was definitely a keeper! Soooo rich, thick and delicious. Don't skip the part where you roast the vegetables first before adding to the pot; it's cooking them this way which really gives the flavour and makes them all caramelised and yummy. As for the recipe name? Suzy is the beautiful dog we were also looking after, who never left my side and managed to successfully get under my feet the entire time I was in her owner's kitchen. I think of her fondly every time I make it!

Serves 4 - 6

Ingredients:

¼ large pumpkin, peeled and cut into large dices

1 large orange kumara (sweet potato), peeled and diced

1 brown onion, finely chopped

2 tbsp oil (or more if needed, for roasting)

2 tsp red curry paste

1 tsp fresh ginger, peeled and finely chopped or crushed

1 tsp red chilli paste

½ cup fresh parsley, finely chopped

1 tbsp nacho spice mix (yes, really! This was all I had and it worked perfectly! But if you don't have this you can simply add a teaspoon each of ground cumin, ground coriander and paprika)

4 cups vegan chicken style stock

1 x 400g can coconut milk

Salt and freshly ground black pepper

fresh coriander (cilantro) to garnish

Method:

First, preheat the oven to 180C. Toss the pumpkin, kumara and onion in the oil and season with a good scrunch of salt and pepper. Lay all the veggies in a large roasting dish or tray and bake for around 30 minutes, until they are nice and soft and caramelised. Give them a stir occasionally to prevent sticking.

Once cooked, transfer the vegetables to a large saucepan and add all the rest of the ingredients except the coconut milk and coriander. Bring to the boil, then reduce heat to low and simmer around 20 minutes. Add the coconut milk and gently heat through. Allow the soup to cool a little before transferring it into a blender and process until smooth. Serve, garnished with fresh coriander (cilantro).

Soups

Tum Yum Soup

I adapted this recipe years ago from a Tom Yum Gai recipe, however on becoming vegan I discovered most Tom Yum pastes contained fish. Not to be defeated, I came up with my own vegan version, which I think works very well and to this day is one of the soups I make most often. You can include whatever other vegetables you like, but if you have chilli paste and tomato paste in your pantry, you have Tum Yum Soup at your fingertips! This makes a light, Asian style soup which can be served either on its own, or with cooked rice or noodles. We love slurping it with thick, soft udon noodles, for an enjoyable accompaniment that will warm your heart as well as your belly.

Serves 4

Ingredients:

2 tbsp peanut oil (you can use another oil, but peanut gives the best flavour)

2 spring onions, finely chopped (omit to make the recipe allium-free)

1 tsp fresh ginger, peeled and finely chopped or crushed

1 tsp chopped lemongrass

1 x 400g can chopped tomatoes, or fresh is best if you have them

4 cups water

4 tbsp tomato paste

2 tbsp chilli paste, or more, to taste

3 medium button mushrooms, sliced

½ capsicum, finely chopped

1 medium courgette, cut into diagonal slices

½ head broccoli, cut into small florets

1 cup roughly chopped spinach or silver beet

3 tbsp lime juice (use fresh, or the best quality bottled lime juice you can get, not the cheap stuff, or it won't taste the same)

1 tsp lemon juice

pinch chilli flakes

2 tbsp fresh coriander (cilantro), finely chopped, plus extra for garnish

fresh chilli, sliced very thinly (optional, for garnish)

fresh lime wedges (optional, for garnish)

Method:

In a large pan, heat the peanut oil over medium heat. Add the chopped spring onions, ginger and lemongrass and cook for a couple of minutes, stirring

Soups

Method Continued ...

occasionally. Add in the water, tomato paste, chilli paste and all the prepared vegetables. Next, add the lime and lemon juices to the pan, along with the chilli flakes and chopped coriander and stir all together well. Bring the pan to the boil, then reduce the heat to low and simmer for 15 minutes. Taste for seasoning, adding more fresh lemon juice if required – this gives a stronger flavour and more 'bite'.

Serve, garnished with the extra coriander, chilli and lime wedges.

Soups

Salads

Before we went vegan, salads were quite frankly a bit of an inconvenience. A couple of slices of tomato and cucumber and a few sad lettuce leaves would get thrown together at the last minute, in an attempt to add something healthy to the plate alongside the other things we REALLY wanted to eat. But the instant we became vegan our sad, boring salads became a thing of the past. We've all heard the old clichés about vegans living on salad, and it's true, we do. But what amazing, mouth-watering and colourful dishes they are. The great thing about salads is you can chuck pretty much anything in! Don't be scared to experiment with different flavour, texture or colour combinations; you may just stumble upon something marvellous.

'Aragma' Greek Salad

WHEAT/GLUTEN FREE   GRAIN FREE

This colourful salad is so quick and easy. You don't even have to toss it! People add all sorts of extras to Greek salads, but the traditional formula is much simpler and doesn't contain any lettuce or leafy greens. 'Aragma' is an informal Greek word meaning 'the small joys of life', which these combined flavours of ripe tomato, crisp cucumber and herb-infused olive oil together most certainly are. It also means 'chilling', and this is the perfect salad to enjoy with friends along with fresh bread or pasta, over a long, leisurely lunch. You can by all means cut the dairy-free feta into cubes and scatter it across your salad, but we find there's something rather nice about leaving it whole and breaking into it with a fork, as is the custom.

Serves 2 - 3

Ingredients:

2 - 3 tomatoes, cut into wedges

½ a cucumber, peeled and cut into half-inch thick slices, then cut in half

½ a small onion (we use red, but you can also use brown), thinly sliced into rings

½ a green capsicum, sliced thinly

6 Kalamata (black) olives, left whole

dried oregano

extra virgin olive oil

red wine vinegar (or you can also use balsamic vinegar)

150g dairy-free feta

Salt, to taste

Method:

Prepare the vegetables as above. To make the salad, first place the tomato wedges and cucumber slices together in a shallow bowl. Add the onion rings and capsicum slices on top of the tomato and cucumber, do not mix together. Next, place the olives on top, whole. Sprinkle the salad lightly all over with dried oregano, then drizzle all over again with olive oil and a splash of red wine vinegar, or balsamic if you're using it. Place the square of feta on top of the salad and sprinkle it with oregano, before finishing with another drizzle of olive oil over the feta.

Serve immediately.

Salads

Big Bunny Salad

This delicious explosion of colour takes the stereotypical 'rabbit' food to a whole new level! With nuts, seeds and spices thrown in and tossed around with abandon, it's got everything in that you could possibly want in a salad. The quantities here make a large amount, making it perfect for work lunches or to take to a barbecue or get together. The family won't taste the turmeric or flaxseed either, so you can sneak it in and they'll have no idea how extra specially good it is for them! For us, this is the basic format, but you can adapt it to add whatever nuts, seeds or other goodies you like. You can choose to chop your veggies a little bigger if you wish, however keeping them that little bit smaller ensures a feast with every mouthful!

70 *Serves 6 - 8*

Ingredients:

2 large handfuls baby spinach, or salad greens

1 cup cherry tomatoes, quartered

1 carrot, peeled and diced

half a red capsicum, diced

2 cups red cabbage, shredded

¼ cup nuts or seeds (e.g. walnuts, sunflower and pumpkin seeds)

1 tsp chia seeds

1 tsp ground flax seed

¼ tsp turmeric

¼ tsp freshly ground black pepper

1 x 400g can chickpeas, rinsed and drained

Method:

Put the handfuls of spinach leaves into a large bowl, followed by the other vegetables, nuts, seeds and spices. Rinse the chickpeas thoroughly and drain well to remove excess water. Add to the rest of the salad and toss all together gently, until well combined.

Enjoy with your favourite dressing.

Salads

Easy Picnic Potato Salad

WHEAT/GLUTEN FREE   **GRAIN FREE**

Finding something good to eat when you're out and about can be a pain when you're vegan. Even hot chips are sometimes cooked in contaminated oils, or animal fat, and while more vegan options are becoming available all the time, often you're not able to simply walk in off the street and grab something decent. We learned long ago that the best bet is to be prepared. A few minutes spent at home making something to eat, in order not to get caught out, hungry or out of pocket is well worth the effort. This simple potato salad may not be gourmet but it's really quick and easy to throw together and we often make it when we go out for the day. It's tasty enough to take along to a picnic, barbecue, or pack with you to take hiking. We can vouch there's something rather gratifying about tucking into home-made potato salad when you're half-way up a mountain!

Serves 2 - 4

Ingredients:

6 - 8 small to medium potatoes, peeled and cut into large diced pieces

half a red onion (or you can use spring onion) finely chopped

couple of sprigs chopped fresh parsley

1 large gherkin, finely chopped

3 - 4 tbsp vegan mayonnaise

salt and freshly ground black pepper, to taste

Method:

First, put your diced potatoes into a medium-sized pan of water and bring them to the boil (make sure that the water covers the potatoes). Simmer gently for around 10 minutes until tender but not mushy. Drain the potatoes well and pop them into a large bowl and set aside to cool for 15 – 20 minutes.

Add the chopped onion, parsley and gherkin to the bowl, along with the mayonnaise and mix together gently until well combined. Taste for seasoning and add salt and pepper as needed until you reach the desired taste. Refrigerate until required.

Salads

Herbalicious Potato Salad

WHEAT/GLUTEN FREE   GRAIN FREE   ALLIUM FREE

This is a lovely and quite different twist on the conventional potato salad. Rather than your usual, creamy dressing, it has a fresh, herby coating which provides an intense, Middle-Eastern flavour and can be enjoyed hot or cold. An exotic dish that's perfect for impressing guests, or when you just feel like serving up something a bit special. The combination of chilli, turmeric and ground coriander gives it a pretty decent kick too!

Serves 4, as a side dish

Ingredients:

6 – 8 medium potatoes (depending on size), peeled and cubed

3 tbsp olive oil

2 tsp turmeric

1 tsp ground coriander

1 tsp chilli flakes

3 tbsp lime juice (or more, to taste)

¾ cup fresh parsley, finely chopped

¾ cup fresh coriander (cilantro), finely chopped

¾ cup fresh dill, finely chopped

salt and freshly ground black pepper, to taste

Method:

First, cook the potatoes. Peel and chop into large dices so they're nice and chunky – not too small. Put them in a saucepan with enough water to cover and bring to the boil, over medium-high heat. Reduce the heat once boiling and simmer gently 5 – 10 minutes until tender, checking every few minutes – you want them just fork-tender, not too soft or mushy. Drain well, rinse with cold water and set aside.

If you haven't done so already, chop all the fresh herbs finely and set aside. Heat the oil in a large frying pan over medium heat. Add the turmeric, ground coriander and chilli flakes, along with the lime juice and cook gently, stirring for a couple of minutes, until fragrant. Add in the potatoes and mix well to coat with the spices. Stir in the prepared fresh herbs and cook for five minutes until the potatoes are heated through. Taste for seasoning, adding salt and pepper, or a little extra lime juice as necessary.

Salads

Quick Marinated Mushroom Salad

WHEAT/GLUTEN FREE ALLIUM FREE

Think you don't like raw mushrooms? You will after you try these. This Asian style salad is so quick to whip up and is always a surprising and pleasant addition to the table. The marinade tenderises the mushrooms, which in turn absorb a subtle sesame flavour. The best thing about it is that it's so fast, making it an ideal solution when your meal needs a little 'something else'. Five minutes is all it takes for the marinade to work its magic, however as with any marinade, the longer you leave it, the more tender your mushrooms will be.

Serves 2 – 4 as a side

Ingredients:

5 large button mushrooms (or more, depending on size) sliced, not too thin

1 tbsp olive oil

1 tbsp sesame oil

1 tbsp tamari

Sesame seeds, for garnish

Method:

Wipe the mushrooms carefully using a slightly damp paper towel to remove any surface dirt. Slice them around a centimetre thick and put in a medium-sized bowl. In another small bowl or jug, put in the olive oil, sesame oil and tamari and mix together well, then pour over the mushrooms. It won't look like it's much dressing, but this small amount is all you need. Mix the mushrooms around gently in the dressing for a couple of minutes, until they are all coated. Set aside until ready to serve, turning them occasionally to keep refreshing the dressing.

You can serve after five minutes or leave for up to two hours for the dressing to permeate. Garnish with sesame seeds before serving.

Salads

Welsh Dragon Bowl

OIL FREE · WHEAT/GLUTEN FREE · ALLIUM FREE

To many people, the thought of making a Dragon Bowl sounds about as terrifying as the creature of legend itself. Where do you start? What on earth do you put in one? It looks so complicated! The thing is, there is actually no great mystery. When you look past the mystical name, it is simply a meal in a bowl. There are no rules, no rights or wrongs when it comes to making one. Traditionally, a Dragon Bowl is designed to be made out of whatever you have on hand, comprising of a base of your choice, such as cooked rice, layered with some raw or cooked vegetables, protein and sauce. Try this version, created by Gareth, our very own 'Welsh Dragon', and you'll see how easy it is to become a Dragon Master!

Quantities are approximate, but should make 1 - 2 bowls, according to size

Ingredients:

Cooked rice, noodles or base of your choice

Baby spinach, or salad leaves

1 carrot, peeled and cut into match-sticks

half a capsicum, de-seeded and sliced thinly

4 cherry or grape tomatoes, cut in half

1 radish, thinly sliced

quarter of a cucumber, cut into matchsticks

half an avocado, peeled and sliced

1 cup cooked edamame (fresh-frozen green soy beans) – or you could use tofu

salad sprouts, e.g. alfalfa

thinly sliced spring onion, to garnish

sesame seeds (optional, to sprinkle over the top)

Plus any sauce or dressing of your choice, to serve

Method:

First, prepare all your vegetables. This makes building your bowl a whole lot faster and easier! Next, put your cooked rice or chosen base in the bottom of your bowl, until it's half-full or thereabouts. Now it's time to start adding the vegies. Think of your bowl as a clock-face and start by putting some baby spinach or salad leaves where 12 would be.

Next, place some carrot sticks next to the leaves, where number 1 would be.

Salads

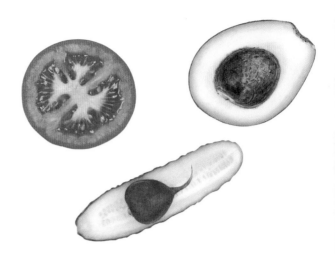

Method Continued ...

From there, add the sliced capsicum at number 2 and keep working your way around, following with tomato, radish, cucumber, avocado, edamame or tofu and sprouts, until you find yourself back at the start. Remember you can modify your bowl to include whatever else you like or have. Finish your beautiful bowl by garnishing with spring onions and sesame seeds, if you're using them.

Serve immediately, with lashings of your favourite dressing. We love this bowl drizzled with our Wasabi Wrecking Ball Dressing (page 235) for a little extra dragon fire!

Everyday Eats

'Everyday eats' can encompass all kinds of things, but they are essentially meals you can put together often, and without much effort. Think of them fondly as your foundation dishes. Meals you can trust on days when everything goes wrong. Dishes you can turn to when you are short on time, money, patience or inspiration. These recipes are all lifesavers, staples and/or lunch ideas, to make eating well through your busy working week that much easier. From burgers to salads, pasta to pizza – even when it comes to turning dinner leftovers into lunch 'bestovers' - we've got you covered.

Almost Egg Burger

CAN BE MADE

WHEAT/GLUTEN FREE | GRAIN FREE | ALLIUM FREE

What do you get when you rub plain tofu lovingly all over with spices and black salt and slap it in a bun? A delicious vegan 'egg' burger. Try this easy recipe and we're sure you'll agree, it tastes even better than the real thing! Perfect for leisurely weekend brunches or breakfast on the go. You can get Himalayan black salt (also known as kala namak) from spice shops and Indian grocers, as well as some supermarkets.

Makes 4 'fried eggs'

Ingredients:

1 x 300g packet firm tofu, drained and pressed

½ tsp turmeric

½ tsp black salt

2 tsp nutritional yeast

4 tbsp oil

Regular or gluten free buns, plus your favourite burger garnishes to serve

Method:

First, carefully cut your block of drained tofu vertically, so you have four 'slabs'. Set aside. Next, mix the turmeric, black salt, nutritional yeast and oil together in a small bowl. Using a brush (or you can use your fingers), coat the slabs of tofu with the oil and spice mixture on both sides, until they are well covered and until the mixture has all been used up. We recommend doing this on a sheet of baking paper or foil, so as not to turn everything yellow! To cook your 'eggs', heat a large frying pan over medium heat. Add the tofu patties and fry for a couple of minutes each side until golden brown and cooked through. You can add a splash of extra oil to the pan if you wish, to prevent sticking. Remove from the pan and place onto a plate lined with paper town to drain any excess oil. Serve as desired, in burger buns, garnished with a fresh, green salad and slathered with your favourite sauce.

Everyday Eats

Bread of Heaven

CAN BE MADE

WHEAT/GLUTEN FREE   ALLIUM FREE

As with many dishes, vegan or non-vegan, it's the sauce which really makes it special and this one is a classic example. It doesn't matter how ordinary or posh the bread is. Even the filling doesn't matter. You can use a swanky store-bought patty or slice up some leftover Beetloaf (page 121). You can add some dairy-free cheese into the mix or leave it out. Whatever you do, it will still taste amazing, thanks to this smoky 'Sweet Southern Sauce', which makes enough for several sandwiches. Be warned, however. Once you try our ultimate toastie, you may well find that nothing else will match up ever again!

Ingredients:

Sweet Southern Sauce

½ cup vegan mayonnaise

2 tbsp tomato sauce

2 tsp farmhouse-style pickle

2 tsp maple syrup

1 tbsp apple cider vinegar

1 tsp smoked paprika

½ tsp garlic powder (optional)

½ tsp onion powder (optional)

salt and freshly ground black pepper, to taste

bread or panini of choice

dairy-free spread

cooked filling, such as leftover Beetloaf (page 121) Neatballs (page 137) or other vegan meat substitute.

lettuce, tomato and / or gherkins to garnish

Method:

Put all the sauce ingredients together in a small bowl and stir well to combine. Taste and season as desired with more salt and pepper if needed. Set aside.

To build your sandwich, first spread the bottom slice of bread with Sweet Southern Sauce. Put your pre-cooked patty or meat substitute on the top, then spread another slice of bread with the sauce and pop that on top, with the sauce side down. Spread the top piece with dairy-free spread.

To cook it, heat a large frying pan over medium heat. Add your sandwich to the pan butter side down, then spread the top piece with more dairy-free spread while in the pan. Cook for a couple of minutes, then flip over and cook the other side, until both sides are golden brown.

Serve hot.

Everyday Eats

Brown and Red Lentil Chilli

OIL FREE   WHEAT/GLUTEN FREE   ALLIUM FREE

This has to be the easiest chilli recipe there is. You don't even have to so much as peel an onion! It's the perfect fast and easy dish to throw together on a weekend to make vegan nachos, or on those nights you really can't be bothered cooking. As with many recipes of this kind, they're even better the next day, so is perfect to make in advance or to enjoy for work lunches.

Serves 4

Ingredients:

¼ cup water

1 large capsicum, finely chopped

1 tbsp chilli powder

1 tsp ground cumin

1 tsp oregano

1 tsp smoked paprika

¼ tsp cayenne pepper

1 x 400g can brown lentils, rinsed and drained

1 cup dried red lentils, rinsed

4 cups vegetable stock

1 x 400g tin tomatoes

1 tsp tamari

1 tsp balsamic vinegar

salt and freshly ground black pepper, to taste

Method:

Heat the water in a large pan over medium-high heat. Add the capsicum and cook gently, stirring occasionally for around five minutes, adding more water if it starts to stick. Add all the rest of the ingredients, stirring well and bring to the boil. Turn the heat down to low and cook, covered for at least 30 minutes (I like to leave it anything up to an hour). Stir occasionally, adding additional water or broth if it gets too thick. Season to taste with salt and pepper.

Serve with corn chips, rice and green vegetables, or salad.

Everyday Eats

Bung-it-in Bolognese

CAN BE MADE

OIL FREE WHEAT/GLUTEN FREE

Everyone has their own way of making 'Spag Bol'. This recipe makes a big pot, with tons of rich flavour and a heap of healthy veggies. As the name suggests, you can experiment with it as much as you like, by bunging in whatever you have. This delicious sauce can be used to make any number of pasta dishes. Leave it nice and chunky, or blitz it a little, so the kids don't realise how many 'greens' they're eating!

Serves 4

Ingredients:

¼ cup water

1 onion, chopped

1 clove garlic, crushed

1 carrot, grated

2-3 mushrooms, finely chopped

2 celery stalks, diced finely

½ head broccoli, chopped very small

1 courgette, finely chopped

2-3 leaves spinach, chopped

2 tbsp fresh parsley, chopped

1 x 400g can chopped tomatoes

1 x 410g can tomato puree

1 x 400g can brown lentils, rinsed well and drained

1 cup beef stock

pinch of chilli flakes

1 tbsp lemon juice (yes, really!)

salt and freshly ground black pepper, to taste

cooked pasta of your choice, to serve.

Method:

Heat the quarter-cup of water in a large saucepan over medium-high heat. Add the onion and garlic and cook for five minutes, stirring occasionally. Throw in the rest of the vegetables, along with the parsley and stir. Add in the canned tomatoes, tomato puree, brown lentils and beef stock and mix all together well, then bring to the boil. Reduce the heat to low, then leave to simmer gently for at least 30 minutes, preferably up to an hour. You can add in extra water, a little at a time if your sauce starts to look too thick. At the end of cooking, add in the chilli flakes and lemon juice and stir well. Taste for seasoning and add salt and pepper if needed.

Serve with cooked spaghetti, or pasta of your choice, accompanied by your favourite dairy-free cheese if you like.

Everyday Eats

Cheat's Mushroom Risotto

WHEAT/GLUTEN FREE

As you can probably tell by the name, this isn't your textbook risotto. We're cheating by using basmati rice instead of the traditional arborio rice, but what the heck, it tastes too good to worry about going against the grain (yes, that pun was intended)! This recipe is super easy and uses just a few simple ingredients yet has so much flavour. The secret is how and when you add the mushrooms. Delicious hot or cold, it's ideal for work lunches or a make-ahead dish for dinner.

Serves 4

Ingredients:

2 - 3 tbsp oil

750g mushrooms, sliced (not too thick, not too thin – and yes, you do need that many!)

scrunch of salt and pepper

2 tbsp dairy-free butter (or more, to taste)

2 cloves garlic, finely chopped or crushed

1 onion, finely chopped

1 ½ cups uncooked long grain rice (we use basmati)

2 ½ cups vegan chicken-style stock

3 spring onions, sliced

Method:

Heat two tablespoons of the oil in a large saucepan over medium-high heat. Add HALF the mushrooms, along with a generous sprinkle of salt and freshly ground black pepper and cook, stirring for around five minutes. Remove from the pan and set aside until the END.

Add the other tablespoon of oil to the pan, along with the butter and stir. Once melted, throw in your garlic and the chopped onion and cook for a couple of minutes before adding the other half of the mushrooms. Cook for five minutes, stirring occasionally. Don't worry if the bottom of the pan goes all brown, that's a good thing and will add more flavour to your dish.

Add your rice to the pan and mix in well, then pour in the stock. Bring everything to the boil, then cover with a lid and reduce the heat to low. Leave to cook gently for

Everyday Eats

Method Continued ...

15 minutes, stirring occasionally to prevent sticking, until all the liquid has evaporated into the rice. You want the rice to be tender but not mushy.

Remove the pan from the heat, then throw in your sliced spring onions, along with the mushrooms you set aside at the start. Stir quickly to combine, then cover the pan again and leave to sit (off the heat) for a further 10 minutes. After 10 minutes, remove the lid, fluff the rice using a fork and taste for seasoning, adding more dairy-free butter if necessary.

Serve immediately.

Creamy Miso Dip for Veggie Sticks

WHEAT/GLUTEN FREE   ALLIUM FREE

This sumptuous dip is so quick-to-make, and will instantly turn any plain, raw vegetable into something super delicious and decadent. This recipe makes a generous amount and once made, it will keep in an airtight container in the fridge for up to five days. Handy to pack in a lunch box with some raw vegie sticks, or to magically bring out as part of a platter when guests pop round unexpectedly!

Serves 4, or more

Ingredients:

¼ cup vegan mayonnaise

¼ cup miso paste

2 tsp cooking sake

2 tbsp rice vinegar

Method:

Put all the ingredients together in a small bowl. Mix well, until the miso paste is thoroughly blended, and you have a smooth dip, with no lumps. Refrigerate until required. Serve with raw vegetables such as carrot, celery, cucumber and capsicum, or you can also pour over salad.

Everyday Eats

Crispy Tofu

WHEAT/GLUTEN FREE   ALLIUM FREE

We should really call this recipe 'tofu for people who don't like tofu'. Like many people who claim to, I used to hate tofu - until Gareth started cooking it this way. Now it's one of our very favourite dishes and is almost always the requested meal on nights when we can't be bothered going to a lot of trouble. Golden, light and crunchy, enjoy these tasty morsels in a Dragon Bowl, with salad and fries, or our favourite, with a selection of Asian dipping sauces.

Serves 2 - 4

Ingredients:

300g firm tofu, drained and pressed

cornflour for coating

oil for frying

Clean, reusable bag or container for shaking

Method:

First, drain and press your tofu to remove any excess liquid. Cut the drained tofu into small, bite-sized cubes and pop the cubes into the bag or container. Cover with cornflour and shake until the tofu is well coated. Cover the base of a large frying pan with oil and heat over a medium high heat. Carefully add the tofu to the pan and fry until golden and crisp, turning regularly as you go. Remove from the pan and drain on a plate or bowl lined with paper towel to remove any excess oil.

Serve as desired.

Everyday Eats

Gareth's Favourite Salad Sandwich

When Gareth first went vegan, like a lot of people he didn't know what he was supposed to eat for lunch any more. So one day I made him a salad sandwich. 'What are you doing?' he asked in alarm. 'Do you want one sandwich, or two?' I replied. 'Only one – what if I don't like it?' he insisted, thinking surely a 'plain' salad sandwich couldn't possibly taste any good without the mandatory meat and cheese? To his surprise, he loved it, and would now eat it every day if he could. If you think a salad sandwich sounds boring, or you've never had one, you need to try this combination. If it can win a former cheese-loving carnivore like Gareth over, it's got to be a winner!

Ingredients:

bread of your choice

hummus

vegan mayonnaise

2 tsp LSA (equal quantities of ground linseed, sunflower seed and almond) or you can use ground flaxseed on its own

lettuce (or you can use baby spinach, or salad greens of your choice)

red onion, finely sliced

sliced tomato

sliced cucumber

avocado, cut into slices

sliced gherkin

pickled jalapeños, finely chopped

sweet chilli sauce

Method:

Spread one slice of bread with hummus, and the other with vegan mayonnaise. Sprinkle the mayo slice with LSA, then place the lettuce on top. Add the red onion, tomato, cucumber and avocado, followed by the gherkin and jalapeños. To finish, drizzle lightly with sweet chilli sauce and pop the other slice of bread on top. Eat! You can of course modify the ingredients to include whatever you like.

Everyday Eats

Garlic-Free Hummus

WHEAT/GLUTEN FREE   GRAIN FREE   ALLIUM FREE

Not everybody likes garlic, and a surprising number of people can't eat it. This makes it very difficult at social get togethers where everyone invariably rolls out the hummus dips, or when you just feel like a dollop of the stuff slathered on some crackers for a quick snack. When I was told I had to stop eating garlic, I was mortified. One thing was for sure though, I wasn't giving up my hummus. I got to work on making a garlic-free version and was amazed to find, not only is it just as delicious, I haven't come across anyone else who doesn't think so either. Trust me, you won't miss a thing. Just make sure not to drain your chickpeas at the start, as you want to save a little of the liquid, so your hummus won't be too dry.

102 *Serves 4*

Ingredients:

1 x 400g can chickpeas (important, do not drain!)

2 tbsp water

2 tbsp lemon juice

1 tbsp olive oil

4 tbsp tahini

2 tsp ground cumin

½ tsp paprika

½ tsp salt

Method:

Spoon the chickpeas into a medium-size bowl or jug, so that you get a little of the liquid going in with them at the same time. Add the rest of the ingredients into the bowl, then using a stick blender (or you can use a regular blender), blitz it until completely smooth. Taste for seasoning, adding more salt, lemon juice or spice if needed, until you achieve the desired flavour.

Serve immediately, or transfer into a sealed container, where it will keep in the fridge for up to five days.

Everyday Eats

Hellagood Pizza

CAN BE MADE

WHEAT/GLUTEN FREE   ALLIUM FREE

We love getting delicious, freshly made takeaway pizza from our favourite pizza outlet. What we don't love is how much it costs every time. Fortunately, thanks to this recipe we can enjoy them as often as we like, for a fraction of the price. If you've got a good dough recipe it's simple; you just make this base at home and add all the same toppings you normally do from your favourite takeaway option. Seriously, this dough will never let you down. If we can make it, anyone can! You can make it as plain or as fancy as you like, either way the effort is so worth it. Better still, it can fast track you to more hassle-free dinners in the future. Just wrap any portions of leftover dough in the freezer and simply defrost and roll it out when you want to make a quick, easy meal.

Makes 4 large pizzas

Ingredients:

Pizza Dough

2 tsp dry yeast

1 tsp sugar

1 ½ cups warm water

3 cups plain regular or gluten-free flour

1 tsp salt

3 tbsp olive oil

Topping

olive oil
(for brushing the pizza base)

tomato paste

grated dairy-free cheese

Other toppings of your choice.

Some of our favourite vegan toppings include -

refried beans

avocado

tomatoes (fresh and sundried)

onion (optional)

capsicum

jalapeños

mushrooms

olives

spinach

cashews

pine nuts

gherkin

sweet chilli sauce

vegan feta

Everyday Eats

toppings continued:

BBQ sauce

fresh coriander (cilantro)

basil

oregano

And of course, the hotly debated pineapple.
Use your imagination!

Method:

First, mix the yeast, sugar and warm water together in a small bowl and let stand in a warm place for a few minutes. Next, put the flour, salt and olive oil into a separate large bowl. Pour in the yeast mixture and then using a metal spoon or butter knife, stir the mixture together until you have a soft dough. Place the dough onto a floured surface and begin kneading for around five minutes. Grease another, large bowl with either oil or dairy-free spread and place your ball of dough in the bowl. Cover it with cling wrap (I like to grease my cling wrap too, so that it doesn't stick to the dough when you go to take it out). Leave your dough in a warm spot for 45 minutes or so, or until it has doubled in size.

Once the dough is ready, divide it into four equal portions. Roll them out on a floured surface, one at a time, into a circle (or as close as you can get to being pizza-shaped!) Carefully lift onto a large oven tray lined with baking paper. Prick the dough all over with a fork. Preheat the oven to 200C. While the oven is heating up, you can get on to preparing your toppings. First, brush the dough all over with olive oil. Next, spread over the tomato paste until the whole surface is covered. Sprinkle over some of the grated cheese. Now, get creative with the rest of your toppings! Finish with more grated cheese, and/or cubes of vegan feta. Place in the oven and cook for around 20 – 25 minutes, or until the pizza is cooked through and golden.

Everyday Eats

Milford Sound Mexican Quinoa Salad

OIL FREE   WHEAT/GLUTEN FREE

A few years back, on a visit to the stunning Milford Sound, we were pleasantly surprised to discover the only cafe there served vegan food, 100km out in the middle of nowhere. I grabbed a Mexican Quinoa Salad to go and was amazed by the awesome and intense combination of flavours in that plain looking takeaway container. I vowed I would recreate it for myself and it took time, but I finally managed to nail it. This version makes a huge amount so is perfect for BBQs and pot luck get togethers, or for your work lunch all week!

Serves 8, or more

Ingredients:

1 cup quinoa (we use white)

1 ½ cups vegetable stock

1 red onion, finely diced

2 large tomatoes, seeds removed and finely diced (you don't HAVE to remove the seeds but would recommend, as it makes for a less soggy salad)

1 large, firm avocado, cut into small dice

1 x 400g tin black beans, well rinsed and drained

1 x 400g tin sweetcorn, rinsed and drained

¾ cup fresh coriander (cilantro), finely chopped

1 - 2 tsp red chilli paste

2 - 3 tbsp lime juice

Salt and freshly ground black pepper to taste

Method:

First, put the vegetable stock into a saucepan. Add the quinoa and bring to the boil over medium heat. Once boiling, reduce the heat to low and cover the pan tightly with a lid. Simmer for 15 minutes or until tender. Set aside.

In a large bowl, put in the chopped onion, tomatoes and avocado. Next, add the black beans and sweet corn, along with the coriander. Mix all together gently, then stir through the chilli paste (I recommend starting with one teaspoon, you can always add more if you want it spicier). Fluff the cooked quinoa with a fork, then add to the bowl and mix thoroughly. Season to taste with salt, pepper and plenty of lime juice. Refrigerate until required. The longer you leave it, the more the taste develops and the better it gets!

Everyday Eats

Spicy Black Beans

WHEAT/GLUTEN FREE   GRAIN FREE

This handy little bean recipe is SO fast to cook and prepare. It's a really useful one to keep in mind when you want to jazz up a simple meal, or are staring blankly into the pantry, wondering what you can conjure up with a few basic ingredients. Perfect for lunches, side dishes, salads, wraps, tacos – pretty much anything!

Serves 4

Ingredients:

1 tsp oil

2 garlic cloves, finely chopped or crushed

half an onion, finely chopped

1 x 400g tin black beans, drained and rinsed

1 tsp ground cumin

1 tsp chilli powder

½ tsp oregano

½ tsp ground coriander

½ tsp paprika

1 tbsp lime juice

¼ cup water

Salt, to taste

Method:

Heat the oil in a frying pan over medium heat. Add the onion and garlic and sauté for 5 minutes, until softened. Add all the other ingredients to the pan, including the water and stir gently to combine. Cook, stirring, until the beans are heated through and the liquid has evaporated. Remove from heat. The result? Delicious, healthy and spicy-coated beans! Once cooked you can serve these over a salad, in tacos, in a wrap – whatever you like. We love them with salad accompanied by fresh chunky guacamole. They taste just as good cold too!

Everyday Eats

Super Easy Brown Lentil Curry

WHEAT/GLUTEN FREE   GRAIN FREE   ALLIUM FREE

This recipe is so straightforward and hassle free. Ideal for busy people or those nights when you really don't feel like cooking. Simply throw it all together and stir! Serve it up with rice, poppadums, a fresh, crispy salad and mango chutney and you've got yourself a delicious meal the whole family will love.

Serves 3 - 4

Ingredients:

2 tbsp oil

1 tbsp cumin seeds

1 tbsp whole coriander seeds (these, along with the cumin seeds really make a difference)

2 tsp fresh ginger, finely chopped or crushed

1 tbsp turmeric

1 tsp cayenne pepper

2 x 400g cans chopped tomatoes

2 x 400g cans brown lentils, drained and rinsed

1 cup coconut milk

salt and freshly ground black pepper, to taste

fresh coriander (cilantro), to garnish

Method:

Heat the oil in a large pan over medium-high heat. Add the cumin and coriander seeds and fry gently for around a minute until they start to sizzle nicely. Add the ginger to the pan, along with the turmeric and cayenne and cook another couple of minutes. Add the tomatoes and drained lentils to the pan and stir well. Bring everything to the boil, then reduce the heat to low and simmer for around 30 minutes, stirring occasionally. Add the cup of coconut milk and bring back to the boil. Taste for seasoning, adding salt and pepper as required, then remove from the heat and serve, garnished with plenty of fresh coriander (cilantro).

Everyday Eats

The Hairy Welshman's Vegan Ramen

Instant noodles needn't be lazy or junk food! We first fell in love with ramen after binge watching *The Hairy Bikers' Asian Adventure* series on TV. Instead of staring wistfully at the screen and thinking 'Wish we could make that', we got off our bums and spent the best part of 12 months experimenting, veganising and living on nothing but Asian food. Asian cuisine combines so many beautiful flavours with such love and care, you can create some wonderful dishes using the humble dried noodle. Here is Gareth's simple but very rewarding recipe for creating the perfect ramen broth. It needs time to simmer, so it can be at its best, but the result is so worth it. Better still, any leftover broth will keep up to five days in the fridge, so be sure to keep some extra noodles in the pantry for a quick and delicious lunch.

Makes 4 servings of broth – uses one noodle cake per serving

Ingredients:

Broth

1 tbsp oil

1 onion, cut into quarters

3 cloves garlic, finely chopped

1-inch piece fresh ginger, peeled and coarsely chopped

5 cups vegetable stock (or you can use vegan chicken style stock)

2 tbsp tamari

1 tbsp miso paste

1 tsp sesame oil

1 – 2 handfuls dried mushrooms

Noodles and Toppings

1 carrot, peeled and cut into matchsticks

1 spring onion, finely chopped

1 small head bok choy per person, leaves separated

instant ramen noodles - one 60g packet per person

1 tsp sesame oil

Method:

Heat a large pot over medium-high heat and add the oil.

Add the onion and fry for a couple of minutes until it starts to soften.

Add in the garlic and ginger and fry gently until aromatic, this should only take a minute or two.

Everyday Eats

Method Continued ...

Pour in the vegetable stock, along with the tamari, miso paste and sesame oil and bring it all to the boil.
Reduce the heat to low and add the dried mushrooms.
Cover the pan with a lid and leave the broth to simmer away gently for at least an hour if possible. The longer you leave

it the better! We recommend a couple of hours, if you have the time. You don't need to prepare your toppings until you are almost ready to cook your noodles.

Around 10 minutes prior to eating, slice the carrot and spring onion.
Bring a pan of water to the boil and cook your noodles as per packet recommendations, then drain well and set aside. In a separate small pan, pour in one teaspoon of sesame oil and sauté the bok choy for a couple minutes at high heat, just enough to soften the stems.

Now it's time to assemble your ramen bowls. You can strain the broth if you prefer but we like to keep all the goodness in ours! Place a serving of drained noodles into each bowl, then ladle in a good amount of broth. Place the bok choy on top of the mound of noodles and sprinkle your carrots and spring onions over. Serve immediately.

Everyday Eats

Feeding the Family

There's this enormous misconception about vegan food, that it only consists of lightweight offerings which can't possibly satisfy the average hungry adult appetite. Which is why Gareth was one of the last people on earth we would ever have picked to go vegan. He, like many others who have gone before him, truly believed he would starve without meat or cheese. To give you an example, a simple pasta bake was lacking for Gareth if it didn't contain at least half a kilo of full fat molten goop. But part of the huge joy of vegan foods is the discovery of new flavours and the enormous scope for experimentation. All the recipes in this chapter have come about through experimenting with new flavours and setting ourselves the challenge to see if we could veganise some of our old family favourites. Not only did we manage to do that, we improved on them to make them healthier, without compromising any of the taste. These recipes have been tested on everyone from fussy youngsters, to seniors, to hungry working blokes and even farmers. All of them have been met with surprise and full, happy bellies. We hope your family enjoys them, too.

Beetloaf

OIL FREE · WHEAT/GLUTEN FREE · ALLIUM FREE

This recipe was a gloriously happy accident when the burger recipe we were originally working on went disastrously wrong. It was never going to work as a patty - but as a loaf mix? It worked like a dream. Not only that, it turned out better than any other vegan 'meat' loaf we have ever tried, both flavour and texture wise. You'll be amazed at how realistic it looks too, served up in the traditional manner with mashed potato and veggies! This recipe makes one large family size loaf, or three small individual size ones. It keeps extremely well in the refrigerator, so is excellent for work lunches throughout the week.

Serves 6

Ingredients:

1 cup cooked quinoa

1 x 400g can cannellini beans, drained and rinsed

1 x 400g can brown lentils, drained and rinsed

1 carrot, grated

1 cup tinned beetroot, drained well

1 cup spinach leaves

1 cup chickpea flour

¼ cup chia seeds

3 tsp mixed herbs

3 tbsp tomato paste

2 tbsp tomato sauce

1 tbsp balsamic vinegar

2 tbsp vegan chicken style stock powder

¾ tsp salt

½ tsp freshly ground black pepper

Glaze

1 tbsp brown sugar

2 tbsp tomato sauce

Method:

First, cook the quinoa according to packet directions and drain well to remove excess moisture. Set aside for 10 minutes or so to cool slightly. Once cooled, put the quinoa into a food processor, along with all the ingredients except for the glaze. Blitz all together until well combined.

Preheat the oven to 200C and grease or line a loaf tin with baking paper. Using a spatula, scrape out as much of the mixture as possible into the loaf tin and smooth over the top (don't worry if it goes a little over and above the fill line).

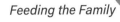

Feeding the Family

Method Continued ...

In a separate, small bowl, mix the brown sugar and tomato sauce together into a paste, then spread across the top of the Beetloaf until it is all used up. Place the loaf into the oven and bake for 35 minutes, or until a skewer comes out clean when inserted into the middle. Remove from the oven and allow to rest for 10 – 15 minutes before turning out. When cool enough to handle, cut into slices and serve.

Feeding the Family

Dragon's Egg(plant)

Power to the purple! This recipe is Welsh in origin and a little bit fiery, just like its inventor! Gareth came up with it when he wanted to create a way of eating tacos which didn't result in everything falling out and making a heck of a mess. He succeeded, and the result was good enough to enjoy on its own. It's eggplant for people who don't like eggplant – or at least think they don't. Delicious in a soft taco the way it was intended, it can also be served as a stand-alone main with salad, vegetables or rice. You can even plonk a slice or two in a wrap, toastie or sandwich; its seasoning makes it so versatile. The name is also a inspired way to get the kids to eat eggplant. Give it a go, you will be pleasantly surprised.

Serves 4

125

Ingredients:

2 whole eggplants, sliced length-wise, approximately ½ inch thick

Spice Marinade

2 tsp taco seasoning mix (available from supermarkets)

3 tsp ground cumin

2 tsp paprika

3 tsp tamari

½ tsp cocoa powder

2 tbsp tomato paste

5 tbsp olive oil

Method:

First, slice both eggplants lengthwise, into approximately six large slices per eggplant. Mix all the spice marinade ingredients into a small bowl. Spread the marinade over both sides of the eggplant slices, covering the flesh only, you don't need to worry about the skin. Set aside and leave for at least an hour, for the flavour to develop.

Preheat the oven to 210C. Line a large baking tray with baking paper and place the eggplant slices onto the tray. Place into the oven and back for 35 minutes, turning the slices over halfway. Remove from the oven and serve in tacos or as desired.

Easy Beany Enchiladas

CAN BE MADE

OIL FREE | GLUTEN FREE | ALLIUM FREE

Ohhh, these really are delicious! They're also a great choice for work lunches as they reheat so well. Despite having multiple components, each is as simple as the next, making it a matter of just bringing it all together. Traditionally, you see enchiladas smothered in grated cheese over the tomato-based sauce, and by all means you are welcome to do that. However, trust us when we say the tahini sauce really adds an extra something special, especially if you want to impress guests! Works well with gluten free wraps too.

Serves 4

Ingredients:

Enchilada Sauce

1 x 400g can tomato puree

1 tsp chilli powder

small pinch cayenne pepper

pinch of salt and black pepper

Enchilada Filling

splash of water, for light cooking

1 whole red capsicum, diced

1 jalapeño, finely chopped

1 ½ tsp ground cumin1 x 400g can black beans, drained and rinsed

¼ cup water (or more as required, if your mixture gets too dry)

2 cups spinach, roughly chopped

4 large tortilla wraps

sliced spring onion, avocado and extra chopped jalapeños, to garnish (optional)

Tahini Sauce

¼ cup tahini

4 tsp cold water

1 tbsp tamari

¾ tbsp maple syrup

1 tbsp Dijon mustard

Method:

First, mix the enchilada sauce ingredients together in a medium bowl and set aside. Heat a splash of water in a large frying pan over medium heat. Add the diced capsicum and jalapeño and sauté gently for a few minutes before adding the cumin and cooking for another minute, stirring. Add in the drained black beans, along with the quarter-cup of water and mix well. Bring to the boil,

Feeding the Family

Method Continued ...

then lower the heat and stir in the spinach. Cook for a couple of minutes, just enough to wilt the spinach and allow the liquid to almost completely evaporate, then remove the pan from the heat. Preheat the oven to 200C. Cover the bottom of a medium-sized baking dish or foil dish with a little of the enchilada filling. Divide the bean mixture into four, equal parts and spoon it down the middle of each tortilla wrap. Roll up the tortillas one at a time, then place into the baking dish, with the seam sides down. Top with the rest of the spicy tomato sauce, so that the wraps are nicely covered. Bake for 15 – 20 minutes, then remove from the oven and set aside for five minutes or so, to rest. While the enchiladas are cooking, make the tahini sauce. Simply put the tahini, water, tamari, maple syrup and Dijon mustard together in a bowl, and whisk briskly with a fork until smooth.

To serve, drizzle the tahini sauce over the top of the cooked enchiladas and serve, garnished with the spring onion and avocado slices and fresh, chopped jalapeños if desired.

Feeding the Family

Marinated Herby Tofu 'Steaks'

WHEAT/GLUTEN FREE   ALLIUM FREE

Never underestimate the belly-filling power of tofu. This simple but moreish recipe is a great one to have on hand when you need to feed a hungry household after a busy day. Just let the tofu sit in the marinade while you prepare some veggies or a salad to go with it, then pop it in the oven and bake until golden. Before you know it, you've got yourself a healthy and substantial meal.

Serves 2 - 4

Ingredients:

Marinade

4 tbsp tamari

2 tbsp olive oil

2 tbsp water

2 tsp rice vinegar

1 tsp dried basil

1 tsp fresh rosemary, finely chopped (or you can use dried)

1 tsp oregano

salt and freshly ground black pepper, to taste

1 block firm or extra firm tofu, drained and pressed

Method:

First, whisk all the marinade ingredients together in a small bowl, then transfer to a large container. Drain and press your tofu thoroughly, to remove as much moisture as possible. Put the block of tofu on its side, then using a sharp knife or cleaver, carefully slice the tofu lengthways into four 'slabs' of even thickness. Place the slabs into the container of marinade and either shake the container, or rub the marinade into the tofu to coat as well as possible. Set aside and leave for 30 minutes, turning the slabs over half way through the cooking process.

Preheat the oven to 200C and line a baking tray with baking paper. Place the tofu slabs onto the baking paper and pour over any remaining marinade. Bake in the oven for 35 minutes, turning half way through cooking. Remove from the oven and serve, either with a fresh salad, or vegetables of your choice.

Feeding the Family

Mexican Lasagne

CAN BE MADE

WHEAT/GLUTEN FREE

This recipe is a brilliant twist on the usual Italian lasagne. It uses tortillas instead of pasta and is so easy to make, with no lengthy simmering of sauces. It's also one of those dishes which isn't obviously vegan, so is a great one for serving up to people who think they won't like vegan food or who think that it's all twigs and leaves. You can easily make it gluten-free too, by using gluten-free tortillas. Without a doubt one of our favourites, we've yet to meet anyone else who doesn't love it too!

Serves 4

Ingredients:

6 - 8 regular or gluten-free tortillas (or more, depending on size)

Black Bean Filling

¼ cup water

1 onion, finely chopped

2 cloves garlic, finely chopped or crushed

2 x 400g cans black beans, rinsed and drained

½ cup fresh coriander (cilantro), chopped

¼ cup dairy-free cheese, grated

Spicy Tomato Sauce

1 x 400g can tomato puree

1 tsp chilli powder

small pinch cayenne pepper

pinch of salt and pepper

Toppings

1 cup dairy-free cheese, grated

½ - 1 avocado, sliced

fresh coriander (cilantro) - optional

Method:

Put the water into a medium saucepan over medium heat. Add the onion and garlic and cook gently for a few minutes, until softened. Add in the two cans of drained black beans, along with the coriander and dairy-free cheese and mix well. Bring to the boil, then reduce the heat to low and let it simmer for 10 minutes, stirring occasionally, then remove from the heat.

Next, make the spicy tomato sauce. Put the tomato puree into a small bowl, along with the chilli powder, cayenne, salt and pepper. Mix well to combine.

Grease a large ovenproof dish or casserole with oil or dairy-free spread. Use 2 – 3 of

Feeding the Family

Method Continued ...

the tortillas to cover the bottom of the dish (or more, as required), then spread some of the spicy tomato sauce over the top. Spread half of the black bean filling on top of that, then repeat the steps with more tortillas, followed by more black beans. Keep stacking until you run out of filling. To finish, pour over the rest of the spicy tomato sauce and sprinkle thickly with dairy-free cheese.

Preheat the oven to 350C. Place the dish into the oven and bake for 15 minutes, until the cheese is melted, and the top is golden-brown. Serve, garnished with extra coriander and slices of fresh avocado.

Meatballs

CAN BE MADE

OIL FREE   WHEAT/GLUTEN FREE   ALLIUM FREE

There are many ready-made vegan 'meatballs' you can buy, but it's far cheaper and more rewarding to make them yourself from scratch. So easy, too! This recipe is incredibly versatile. Herby and 'meaty' in texture, you can add them to pretty much anything. You can make them gluten-free too, by using gluten-free breadcrumbs, available from supermarkets, and a basic gluten-free flour, such as rice flour. Enjoy them in traditional pasta dishes, for lunch in wraps, with dipping sauces, even with mashed spuds, veggies and gravy. Oven-baked or shallow fried, you can't go wrong with them.

Makes up to 45 'meatballs', depending on size

Ingredients:

1 x 400g tin black beans, drained and rinsed

1 x 400g tin cannellini beans, drained and rinsed

3 tsp mixed herbs (or you can use a mixture of dried thyme, oregano and basil)

3 cups regular or gluten-free breadcrumbs

Method:

Put all the ingredients together in a large bowl. Using a stick blender (or you can use a food processor), whizz everything up until nice and mushy. If the mixture seems a little too wet, you can add more breadcrumbs or a little plain or gluten-free flour, such as rice flour if required. Line a large oven tray with baking paper. Use heaped teaspoons of mixture to form into small balls and place onto the tray. To cook, either bake in the oven at 200C for 20 minutes, or shallow fry in a large frying pan over medium heat for around 10 minutes, turning occasionally. Serve as desired.

Feeding the Family

Potato Hedgehogs

These fancy baked potatoes are nothing short of magic. They taste just as though you are eating a bacon and cheese potato, yet there is not a scrap of bacon or cheese in them! It's worth going to the little extra effort to make these special spuds the whole family will love.

Serves 4

Ingredients:

4 large baking potatoes, scrubbed clean, skins on

½ cup dairy-free milk (almond or soy works well)

3 tbsp vegan mayonnaise

2 tsp smoked paprika

2 tsp garlic powder

2 tsp onion powder

1 tsp salt

freshly ground black pepper, to taste

Method:

Preheat the oven to 200C for 10 minutes. Place the potatoes in the oven on a baking tray and bake for between 40 – 60 minutes (depending on size) until tender, turning over half way. Remove from the oven and set aside until cool enough to handle. Using a small, sharp knife, cut a slice off the top of each cooked potato, and scoop out the flesh, so you have potato 'cups'. Put the discarded potato flesh into a separate bowl.

Add the dairy-free milk, mayonnaise, smoked paprika, garlic powder, onion powder, salt and pepper to the potato flesh in the bowl and mash all together well, until smooth. Fill the potato cups back up again with the creamy mash mixture and fluff the tops with a fork, to resemble 'spikes'. Sprinkle the top with a little extra smoked paprika.

Turn the oven back on to 180C and pop the potatoes back in for another 10 minutes to heat up.

Serve immediately.

Feeding the Family

Reggie's Veggies

WHEAT/GLUTEN FREE   GRAIN FREE

This heart-warming, filling vegetable dish is named after Reggie, a delightfully bonkers and very energetic pup we were looking after during the coldest and bleakest time of the year. It's tasty, it's colourful and makes a nice and very welcome change from the usual winter.veg. You can either serve it as a side dish, or as the main part of your meal. Feel free to jazz it up however you like with additional root vegetables, such as parsnip, or add a little extra zing with a pinch of cayenne pepper.

Serves 4

Ingredients:

1 tbsp oil

2 medium onions, quartered

3 carrots, peeled and diced

1 x 400g tin chopped tomatoes

2 tsp vegan Worcestershire sauce

6 medium potatoes, cut into large dice

salt and freshly ground black pepper, to taste

fresh parsley, to garnish (optional)

Method:

Heat the oil in a large saucepan over medium heat. Add the onions and sauté them for several minutes until golden, stirring occasionally. Add the carrots and stir, then add in the tomatoes and Worcestershire sauce, mixing again to combine. Bring to the boil, then reduce heat to low and cook for 30 minutes. Add the diced potatoes to the pan, along with plenty of salt and pepper and stir well. Cook for another 30 minutes, or until all the vegetables are tender, stirring frequently to prevent burning. Serve hot, garnished with fresh parsley.

Feeding the Family

Sheep Friends' Pie

WHEAT/GLUTEN FREE   GRAIN FREE

Some recipes are easy to veganise, others are not. When I was growing up, my Mum made the best Shepherd's Pie ever, and her recipe was handed down to me. Upon going vegan, I thought adapting it would be as simple as swapping the usual mince for a can of nutmeat. I was wrong; it was so bad it was almost inedible! So we went back to the drawing board and after several attempts, Gareth came up with this easy and very tasty version, completely from scratch. We think it's by far the best vegan, sheep-friendly pie we have ever had. We hope you enjoy it too.

Serves 6 - 8

Ingredients:

Filling

3 cups water

2 vegan beef style stock cubes

1 block firm tofu

1 tbsp olive oil

1 onion, finely chopped

1 carrot, peeled and grated

1 courgette, grated

1 tsp rosemary, finely chopped

2 tsp oregano

3 tbsp tomato paste

1 x 400g can brown lentils, rinsed and drained

1 tsp Worcestershire sauce

1 tbsp tamari

salt and freshly ground black pepper

Topping

6 – 8 potatoes (depending on size), cooked and mashed

dairy-free spread, for mashing

Splash of dairy-free milk (optional), for mashing

Method:

Place the water and stock cubes into a large pot and bring it to the boil. Crumble the tofu into the stock and allow to simmer gently. In a separate pan, heat the oil over medium heat. Add the onion to the pan and sauté for a few minutes until soft. Add the grated carrot and courgette to the onion, along with the rosemary and oregano and cook for a couple more minutes. Finally, add the tomato paste and drained lentils and mix all together well. Add everything to the tofu and stock, along with the Worcestershire sauce and tamari. Bring back to the boil, then reduce heat

Feeding the Family

Method Continued ...

to low and simmer for 30 minutes. Once cooked, taste for seasoning and season with salt and pepper as required. Transfer the mixture to a large, oven-proof dish or casserole.

Preheat the oven to 200C for 10 minutes. Place your dish of lentil 'mince' into the oven and bake for 30 minutes. This allows the tofu to absorb more of the excess liquid and enables a nice, firm base to spread your topping on.

While the base is cooking, prepare your mashed potato topping. Peel and slice the potatoes and pop them into a large pan of water, enough to cover them. Bring to the boil over a high heat, then reduce the heat and simmer for around 15 minutes, or until the potatoes are tender enough so that a knife skewers them easily, without resistance. Drain well and mash, adding a little dairy-free spread and/or plant milk, until smooth and creamy. You just want to add a little at

a time, so your mash is easy enough to spread, but not sloppy.

Once your topping is cooked, remove from the oven and allow to rest for 5 – 10 minutes before adding the mashed potato. Place it onto the topping, a little at a time so that it doesn't 'sink', spreading and smoothing it out as you go, until the whole base is covered. Pop back into the oven for another 30 minutes, or until the topping is golden brown. Remove from the oven and serve, accompanied by vegetables of your choice.

Feeding the Family

Smoky Sweet Potato Chilli

OIL FREE   WHEAT/GLUTEN FREE

For a warming and filling meal that's as smoky in flavour as it is spicy, look no further than this easy dish. We make it on the stove top but you could easily throw everything in a crockpot and cook it slowly. Serve on its own, or with salad, over rice, or in a soft tortilla bowl.

Serves 4

Ingredients:

1 large onion, finely chopped

3 cloves garlic, finely chopped or crushed

1 large sweet potato (kumara), peeled and diced

1 x 400g four bean mix, rinsed well and drained

1 x 400g can chopped tomatoes

1 cup water (or more, as necessary)

2 bay leaves

2 tsp mixed herbs

2 tsp chilli flakes (or just use one if you prefer it milder)

½ tsp smoked paprika

¼ tsp good quality cocoa powder

salt and freshly ground black pepper

fresh avocado or jalapeños (optional), to garnish

Method:

Put a splash of water in a large saucepan over medium heat. Add the chopped onion and garlic and cook gently for a few minutes until soft. Add in all the other ingredients except the salt and pepper and mix well. Bring to the boil, then reduce the heat to low and simmer, covered, for around 40 minutes. Stir occasionally during cooking, adding more water if the mixture looks too thick until you reach the desired consistency. Test for seasoning and serve with your favourite garnishes. e.g. fresh avocado or sliced jalapeño.

Feeding the Family

Speedy Refried Bean Burger

CAN BE MADE

WHEAT/GLUTEN FREE

Refried beans are a real unsung hero in vegan cooking. Don't limit them to nachos, they're a lot more versatile than you think. If you've got a tin of refried beans in the pantry, you've got yourself a quick and filling meal. This recipe gives you a good basic burger patty that the whole family will love and can be easily modified to include whatever herbs or spices you like. It can easily be made gluten-free too, by using gluten-free breadcrumbs and burger buns. If you can't find gluten-free breadcrumbs, I often make my own fresh ones by simply grating a couple of slices of gluten-free bread and they turn out just as well. If you don't have fresh coriander (cilantro) you can substitute it with a couple of sprigs of fresh parsley.

Makes 4 patties

Ingredients:

1 tbsp oil, for frying

1 x 400g can refried beans

½ – ¾ cup dried regular or gluten-free breadcrumbs
(or 1 cup if you're using fresh)

⅓ cup fresh coriander (cilantro), finely chopped

Flour for dusting

Burger buns (either regular or gluten-free) and your favourite burger toppings to serve.

Method:

Put the refried beans in a bowl with the breadcrumbs and chopped herbs and mix/mash together until well combined. Pop it in the fridge for 30 minutes or so.

Divide the mixture into four equal parts and form into patties, dusting with flour to prevent sticking. Set aside.

Heat the oil in a large frying pan over medium high heat and carefully add the burger patties to the pan. Cook for around three to four minutes each side, turning once, until nice and golden. Remove from the pan and drain on a plate lined with paper towel to remove excess oil.

Serve in buns or as desired. We love dressing ours up with onion, baby spinach, sliced gherkin and vegan mayo, alongside a serving of chunky home-made wedges!

Feeding the Family

Star Wars Stew

What on earth is 'Star Wars Stew?' It's a cheeky little hotpot; a gloriously eclectic slow-cook concoction I've been making since I was knee-high to a grasshopper. The ingredients sound really unlikely but I've yet to meet anyone who doesn't like it. The original version contains sausages and bacon, but not wanting to miss out on this childhood favourite, I developed a vegan version and the results are just as good, if not better. We don't use ready-made products as a rule, but this is an exception, especially if you're in a hurry. If you're not pushed for time and prefer meatballs to sausages, you can also make it with our Neatball recipe, (page 137). This filling stew is a meal in itself but is also delicious served with steamed vegetables.

Serves 4 - 6

Ingredients:

¼ cup water

2 onions, finely chopped

1 x 400g tin baked beans

1 x 400g tin whole kernel sweet-corn, drained

1 x 400g tin chopped tomatoes

1 packet vegan sausages, cut into quarters (or 1 batch cooked Neatballs, as many as you can fit into the pot)

1 whole bay leaf

salt and freshly ground black pepper, to taste

3 - 4 large potatoes, peeled and sliced

grated dairy-free cheese

Method:

Preheat the oven to 180C. In a large, ovenproof pot or casserole, heat the water over medium heat. Add the chopped onion and cook for a few minutes until soft. Throw in the baked beans, sweetcorn and chopped tomatoes. Pop in the bay leaf and season well with salt and pepper. Add in the chopped vegan sausages (or cooked Neatballs, whichever you're using) and gently mix all together. Place the potato slices over the top of the mixture, ensuring it is all covered as much as possible and season again with salt and pepper. Cover the pan with foil and cook in the centre of the oven for 1 ½ hours. Remove the foil and sprinkle over the grated cheese. Increase the oven temperature to 200C and pop the stew back in the oven for another 20 minutes, or until the cheese is melted and the potatoes are tender. Serve steaming hot.

Feeding the Family

Stuffed Mexican Courgettes

WHEAT/GLUTEN FREE · GRAIN FREE · ALLIUM FREE

This is another recipe which demonstrates what a handy addition a can of refried beans can be to your pantry, especially when courgettes (zucchini) are in season. This simple but tasty recipe is one of those great ones which will have everyone thinking you've been spending ages slaving away in the kitchen when you actually haven't at all. Get the kids to help with the scooping and filling part and it's even easier! You can omit the onion and tomato salsa and simply top the refried bean mixture with grated cheese if allium-free, or to make them more kid-friendly. Handy tip – if you have trouble with your courgette halves rolling around on the oven tray, cut a thin slice off the underside so they sit nice and flat.

Serves 4

Ingredients:

4 medium courgettes

1 tbsp olive oil

1 whole, fresh chilli, seeds removed and finely diced

1 x 400g can refried beans (check ingredients to make sure they are vegan)

1 tsp ground cumin

½ – 1 tsp chilli powder

1 large tomato, finely chopped

half an onion, finely chopped

salt and freshly ground black pepper, to taste

1 cup grated dairy-free cheese (optional)

Lime juice and finely chopped fresh coriander (cilantro), to garnish

Method:

First prepare the courgettes by cutting each one in half lengthways and removing the stalk. Using a dessert spoon, carefully scoop out the seeds in each one and discard, to make a sort of hollowed out 'boat'. Make sure when doing this part to leave enough flesh around the edges so the courgette will hold its form and not collapse. Once finished, put the courgette halves onto an oven tray lined with baking paper and set aside.

In a medium-sized saucepan, heat the olive oil over medium heat. Add the diced chilli pepper and sauté a few minutes. Next, add in the refried beans, cumin and half a teaspoon of the chilli powder and mix all together well. Cook, stirring for five minutes, until the mixture is warmed through. Taste for seasoning, adding the rest of the chilli powder if required.

Feeding the Family

Method Continued ...

Divide the bean filling equally to stuff the courgettes (I find this is easiest to do using a teaspoon).

Preheat the oven to 180C. While the oven is heating up, finely chop the tomato and onion and mix together in a small bowl, along with a good scrunch of salt and pepper. Top the stuffed courgettes with the tomato and onion mixture, then finish with the grated cheese. Bake in the centre of the oven for 35 minutes, or until the courgettes are tender, but not mushy. Serve, garnished with a sprinkle of lime juice and fresh chopped coriander.

Sweet and Sour Tofu

WHEAT/GLUTEN FREE

Before we became vegan, Sweet and Sour was our most requested takeaway meal. After making the switch, it was almost too much to hope that we would still be able to enjoy that lip-smacking, sticky sauce with anything else. A little tweak here and there however, and we think our veganised version is even better than the takeaway favourite! It's one of the naughtier recipes in the book, with ¾ cup of sugar lovingly melded into the sauce, but it's a great treat for special occasions or to make a 'Chinese takeaway at home'. Technically this recipe is supposed to serve four people, however Gareth loves it so much he is more than capable of scoffing the lot by himself ...

Serves 4

Ingredients:

Tofu

300g firm tofu, drained and pressed

cornflour for coating

oil for frying

clean reusable bag or container

Sauce

¾ cup sugar

½ cup apple cider vinegar

¼ cup tomato sauce

1 tbsp tamari

½ tsp garlic power

2 tbsp cornflour

2 tbsp water

cooked rice, to serve.

Method:

First, prepare the tofu. Drain and press your tofu block to remove any excess liquid, then cut into small, bite-sized cubes and pop them into the clean bag or container. Cover with cornflour and shake until the cubes are well coated. Cover the base of a large frying pan with oil and heat over a medium high heat. Carefully add the tofu to the pan and fry until golden and crisp, turning regularly as you go. Remove from the pan and transfer into a fairly deep oven proof dish. Set aside while you make the sauce.

To make the sauce, put the sugar, cider vinegar, tomato sauce, tamari and garlic powder into a small saucepan and stir well to combine. Heat the pan over a medium heat until it comes to the boil. Reduce heat and simmer for five minutes, stirring to prevent sticking. In a small bowl or jug,

Feeding the Family

Method Continued ...

mix the cornflour and water together until completely smooth, then gradually add to the saucepan, stirring constantly. Keep cooking and stirring the sauce for a few minutes until you see it begin to thicken and go glossy.

Put the oven on to heat at 180C. Pour the sauce over the prepared tofu in the ovenproof dish until it is completely covered, then place in the hot oven. Bake for 30 minutes, turning over half way to evenly coat the tofu, taking care not to let it burn. Remove from the oven and serve with cooked rice.

Feeding the Family

Ye Olde Family Chilli

WHEAT/GLUTEN FREE

When it comes to cooking and sampling chilli dishes, we both consider ourselves to be somewhat connoisseurs. As a teenager, my love for Chilli con Carne was so great, the chef in the restaurant where I worked bestowed the honour of official chilli taster upon me. As for Gareth, some of his first memories of cooking was making chilli, studying his mother's prizewinning recipe. This is his vegan interpretation of that very recipe, which is still the best we have tasted.

Serves 4

Ingredients:

1 tbsp oil

1 onion, finely chopped

3 cloves garlic, finely chopped or crushed

1 whole capsicum, finely chopped

2 x 400g cans chopped tomatoes

1 vegan beef style stock cube

1 x 400g can red kidney beans, rinsed and drained

1 x 400g can brown lentils, rinsed and drained

1 tbsp cocoa powder

2 tsp ground cumin

1 tsp paprika

1 tsp oregano

½ tsp chilli powder

grated dairy-free cheese, to garnish (optional)

Method:

Heat the oil in a large saucepan over medium heat. Add the onion and garlic and sauté a few minutes, stirring occasionally, until softened. Add in the chopped capsicum, followed by all the rest of the ingredients and stir all together well. Bring to the boil, then reduce heat to low and simmer, covered for around 15 minutes. Serve on its own in a bowl, garnished with dairy-free cheese, with rice, or oven-baked potato with a fresh salad.

Feeding the Family

Entertaining

Vegans love cooking for all kinds of people. Unfortunately, not so many people like cooking for us. It's all too hard, too many questions. What do we EAT? Where do you even get that kind of food FROM? What if I get it WRONG? Here's a reassuring fact, nobody loves food - or a get together that involves food, more than vegans. Entertaining people with specific food requirements doesn't have to be hard or stressful. There is *so much* you can make with plants! Cooking for others provides the opportunity to experiment with new foods and create beautiful dishes. Embrace it by trying some of these all-year-round recipes. They will see you right when visitors suddenly descend, or you are planning to host a houseful. Get stuck in and amaze your guests. Vegan or not, they will love these dishes, and you.

Baked Polenta Fries

WHEAT/GLUTEN FREE · ALLIUM FREE

If you have never tried polenta fries, you need to stop missing out and learn how to make them, right now. This easy-peasy recipe takes the mystery out of polenta and makes a delightful and welcome change from the usual spud fries. Crispy, crunchy and delicately seasoned, these super-size fries are guaranteed to become family favourites. This recipe makes a nice, big batch of chunky fries. You can either make them the main part of a meal for two people or serve them as a side dish. Either way, be sure to dip and dunk them in all your favourite sauces!

Makes 30 – 35 chunky fries

Ingredients:

1 ½ cups polenta (that's cornmeal flour for those who don't know. Do NOT confuse it with cornflour, that's a totally different thing!)

3 cups vegetable stock

2 tbsp olive oil

2 tbsp nutritional yeast

½ tsp paprika

1 tsp fresh parsley

1 tsp fresh rosemary (you could also use dried, or mixed herbs)

salt and freshly ground black pepper, to taste

Method:

First, put the vegetable stock, olive oil, nutritional yeast, paprika, parsley and mixed herbs all together in a large pot (we use a soup pot). Heat over a medium heat and bring to the boil. Once boiling, gradually add in the polenta with one hand, while all the time stirring like mad with the other. Continue beating the mixture until you end up with a very thick mass of polenta, similar to stuffing consistency. Don't worry if you have trouble getting your spoon or spatula through it as it thickens, it's supposed to go like that! Remove from the heat, taste and season as desired with salt and pepper.

Line an 20cm x 20cm (8"x 8") baking dish or similar size with cling wrap. Scrape out all the polenta into the dish. Spread and smooth it all out as best you can until it covers the whole dish. Smooth across the

Entertaining

Method Continued ...

top as much as possible (we find doing this with a rubber spatula works best!) Pop the dish into the fridge to set. Ideally you should chill it for an hour, but as long as the polenta is cold and has firmed up you could do a little less.

Preheat your oven to 190C and line a baking sheet with baking paper. Brush the baking paper lightly with a tiny amount of oil. Turn your polenta out onto a chopping board. By now it should be a nice, firm block. Using a sharp knife, cut the block into fry-like shapes. Place the fries onto the lined baking tray in a single layer. Ideally you don't want them touching each other. Bake for 30 minutes, then turn them over and bake for another 10 minutes. Remove from oven and serve just as you would regular fries, with your favourite sauces or dips. For a truly delicious combination, try them with any of our flavoured mayo's, on page 208.

Big Bucket o' Biryani

WHEAT/GLUTEN FREE

We came up with this recipe on World Vegan Day, when we wanted to make something terribly impressive and gourmet, but our fridge had other ideas. A biriyani is a brilliant way to use up all sorts of bits and bobs and sad-looking veggies. I also love making them as you cook everything together in the one big pot, no mucking around cooking rice separately. You can of course adapt the recipe to use up whatever you have, e.g. swap the peas for beans, add a finely chopped zucchini, whatever you like. As the name suggests, this recipe makes a huge, big pot, so is just the thing for feeding a crowd or making a big batch for work lunches.

Serves 8

INGREDIENTS:

2 tbsp oil

1 onion, finely chopped

2 cloves garlic, finely chopped or crushed

1 sweet potato, peeled and cut into small dice

1 whole capsicum, chopped

2 whole tomatoes, diced

200g peas (canned or frozen)

200g sweetcorn (tinned or frozen)

2 tbsp red curry paste

1 tsp turmeric

1 tsp chilli flakes

500g basmati rice

4 cups vegetable stock

fresh coriander (cilantro), chopped for garnish

cashews (optional) for garnish

METHOD:

In a large pot (e.g. soup or stock pot), heat the oil over medium heat. Add the onion and garlic and sauté for a few minutes until softened. Add the sweet potato, capsicum, tomatoes, peas and corn and cook a few more minutes until softened. Stir in the curry paste, turmeric and chilli flakes until the vegetables are nicely coated. Sprinkle the basmati rice over the top and stir through the mixture, then add the vegetable stock and mix all together well. Bring to the boil, then reduce the heat to low and simmer, covered for around 25 minutes, stirring occasionally until the rice is cooked but not mushy. Serve, garnished with fresh coriander (cilantro) and cashews.

Entertaining

Candlelight Curry

OIL FREE   WHEAT/GLUTEN FREE   GRAIN FREE

It's ridiculous how hard it is to find a good vegetable curry. Almost all the ones we've ever tried have been a huge disappointment. This recipe however is one you'll want to make time and again. It's a basic vegetable korma, which isn't too spicy but is loaded with flavour and never lets you down. We've called it 'Candlelight Curry' as it is classy enough to dish up to someone you want to impress, but down-to-earth enough to make for the family. Serve with rice, pappadums and a peach or mango chutney and you've got yourself a guaranteed hit.

Serves 4

Ingredients:

¼ cup water

1 large sweet potato, peeled and diced

1 onion, finely chopped

½ head cauliflower, cut into small florets

1 tsp fresh ginger, finely chopped or crushed

2 tsp curry powder

1 tsp garam masala

1 tsp ground coriander

1 tsp turmeric

1 x 400ml can coconut cream

3 tsp tomato paste

1 vegetable stock cube

1 x 400g can green beans, drained (or you can use frozen)

1 small can peas, drained (or you can use frozen)

salt and freshly ground pepper, to taste

handful of cashew nuts, to garnish

Method:

Put the quarter-cup of water into a large pan over medium-high heat. Add the sweet potato and cook gently, stirring for a few minutes. Add in the onion, cauliflower and fresh ginger and cook another five minutes, stirring occasionally and adding more water if the vegetables start to stick. Add the curry powder, garam masala, ground coriander and turmeric to the pan and stir. Pour in the coconut cream, followed by the tomato paste and vegetable stock cube, then the beans and peas. Mix all together well to combine. Bring to the boil, then reduce the heat to low and simmer for around 15 minutes, until all the vegetables are tender. Season to taste with salt and pepper and serve, sprinkled with cashews.

Entertaining

Chickpea Flatbreads

WHEAT/GLUTEN FREE   GRAIN FREE   ALLIUM FREE

Chickpea flour is really economical, and a little goes a long way. Also known as 'socca', these delicious savoury darlings are gluten-free and grain-free and were my lifesaver when I learned I was coeliac. You certainly don't have to be gluten-free to enjoy them, though! They are a staple for me but are also good enough to whip up and serve to guests. They are so versatile and can be eaten hot or cold. I love to eat mine topped with mung bean sprouts, with a splash of tamari and a fresh salad. You can top them with anything you like though, from roasted, summer vegetables to garlic mushrooms. Or, you can be like the French and just serve them up with a flourish of freshly ground black pepper. This recipe makes two flatbreads, or one serving, but they freeze really well so you can by all means multiply the mixture to make a bigger

batch for convenience. You can also leave out the chilli flakes and coriander if you prefer them plain, I just like to have them for a nice bit of zing and colour.

Serves 1

Ingredients:

½ cup chickpea flour

large pinch of salt

⅔ cup water

1 – 2 tbsp fresh coriander (cilantro), finely chopped

pinch chilli flakes

4 tbsp olive oil (2 tbsp per flatbread)

Method:

Put the chickpea flour and salt into a medium-sized bowl. Add in the water a little at a time, whisking as you go to remove any lumps. The batter will be very thin by the time you have added all the water. Add the coriander and chilli flakes if you're using them, or leave plain.

When it comes to cooking the flatbreads, it can take a little practice to perfect if you want to avoid a gooey, lumpy mess! This way is what works for me best, I recommend following it to the letter, at least to start with. First, heat two tablespoons of the oil in a small, non-stick frying pan (such as an omelette pan) over a high heat. Once the oil is hot,

Entertaining

Method Continued ...

pour half the batter into the pan and quickly spread it around to cover the bottom by jiggling the pan, as if you were making an omelette. Cook for exactly four minutes on one side only, without turning over, until firm and you can lift around the edges cleanly. Carefully flip over with a large spatula and cook the other side for another 2 – 3 minutes, until the flatbread is golden-brown and cooked through.

Remove from the pan and set aside on a plate lined with paper towel, to drain any excess oil. Repeat the process again by heating the other two tablespoons of oil and adding the other half of the mixture. Serve on its own, or with toppings, or cut into wedges.

Courgettes A La Grecque

WHEAT/GLUTEN FREE · GRAIN FREE · ALLIUM FREE

'A la grecque' means served in a sauce made of olive oil, lemon juice, and several seasonings, just like this one. I first learned this recipe when I was nine years old and still love to make it today. Delicious hot or cold, and rich in colour and flavour, serve this little gem as a side dish or main, accompanied by a fresh salad and crusty bread to mop up all that delicious sauce!

Serves 4

Ingredients:

500g courgettes (around 5 or 6)

salt

¾ cup olive oil

juice of one whole lemon

1 ¼ cups water

1 bay leaf

sprig fresh thyme
(or you can use ½ tsp dried)

1 x 400g tin chopped tomatoes

freshly ground black pepper, to taste

Method:

Chop the courgettes into thick slices, removing the stalks. Sprinkle them with salt and set aside for an hour to drain, covered with a clean tea towel to absorb the moisture. Put the oil into a large saucepan over medium heat. Add the lemon juice, water, bay leaf and thyme and stir. Bring to the boil, then add in the tomatoes and courgettes. Reduce the heat and simmer for 25 - 30 minutes, until the sauce has thickened. Taste for seasoning and add more salt and pepper if needed before serving.

Entertaining

Crispy Tofu Satay Noodle Bowl

WHEAT/GLUTEN FREE

Whoever knew instant noodles could be so classy? We first came up with this recipe one Christmas Day! We wanted a relaxing day and didn't want to go to the effort of making a huge roast dinner just for two of us, so decided to jump in the kitchen and create something instead. This was the result, and we enjoyed it just as much as any other traditional Christmas lunch. It's a great dish to bring out when you need something 'easy but special'. You could make it with pretty much any type of noodle, including gluten-free.

Serves 2 - 4

Ingredients:

1 x 85g packet instant ramen noodles per person (or you can use gluten-free rice noodles)

Crispy Tofu -

300g firm tofu, drained and pressed

cornflour for coating

oil for frying

clean reusable bag or container for shaking

Satay Sauce -

2 spring onions, finely chopped

1 tsp fresh ginger, peeled and finely chopped

2 whole green chillies, seeds removed and finely chopped

2 tbsp fresh coriander (cilantro), finely chopped

¾ cup crunchy peanut butter

3 tsp tamari

300ml coconut cream

4 tbsp lime juice

salt, to taste

100g fresh, whole snow peas, topped and tailed

fresh coriander (cilantro), to garnish

Method:

First, make the satay sauce. Put the spring onions, ginger, chillies, coriander, peanut butter, tamari, coconut cream and lime juice together in a medium bowl or jug. Using a stick blender (or you can transfer all the ingredients to a regular blender), blitz until thick and creamy. Taste for seasoning, adding a little salt if needed. Set aside.

Entertaining

Method Continued ...

Next, prepare and cook the crispy tofu. Drain and press the tofu block to remove any excess liquid. Once drained, cut the block into small, bite-sized cubes and pop the cubes into your clean bag or container. Cover with enough cornflour to coat and shake until the tofu is well covered. Cover the base of a large frying pan with oil and heat over a medium high heat. Carefully add the tofu to the pan and fry until golden and crisp, turning regularly as you go. Remove from the pan and drain on a plate or bowl lined with paper towel. Set aside, keeping warm if possible.

Put two saucepans of water on to heat – one to cook the noodles in and the other for the snow peas. Cook the noodles according to packet directions. Drain and set aside. Bring the other pan of water to the boil, then pop in your snow peas. Bring them back to the boil, then cook for 2 – 3 minutes. Remove from the heat and drain.

To build your bowl, divide the cooked noodles between each bowl. Arrange the cooked tofu and snow peas on top of the noodles. Drizzle with the satay sauce and serve, garnished with fresh coriander (cilantro).

Entertaining

Denise's Beany Salad

WHEAT/GLUTEN FREE   GRAIN FREE

This delicious and colourful dish is perfect when you need to come up with something quick and easy for BBQ's and get togethers that both vegans and non-vegans will love. It was given to us by our friend Denise, who makes it all the time for her non-vegan husband's work lunch. She also made a huge batch to serve to our guests at our fully vegan wedding. Everyone always loves it!

Serves 6 - 8

Ingredients:

1 can four bean mix, rinsed and drained

1 can red kidney beans, rinsed and drained

1 small red onion (or half a large one), finely chopped

½ red capsicum, finely chopped

½ green or yellow capsicum, finely chopped

2 - 3 stalks celery, finely diced or sliced

2 tbsp fresh parsley, chopped (don't use dried; it won't be the same!)

Dressing

⅓ cup olive oil

¼ cup balsamic vinegar

1 tsp brown sugar

1 clove garlic, finely chopped or crushed

large pinch of salt, or to taste

Method:

In a large bowl, combine the drained beans with the chopped onion, capsicums, celery and parsley and mix all together well.

Put the olive oil, balsamic vinegar, brown sugar, garlic and salt together in a small bowl or jug and whisk to combine, then drizzle over the beans and mix together thoroughly. Taste for seasoning, adding more salt if necessary.

Enjoy on its own, in wraps or as a side dish. Keeps well for several days refrigerated.

Entertaining

Kimmie's Greek Potatoes

WHEAT/GLUTEN FREE ALLIUM FREE

These comforting and intensely flavourful potatoes serve as a delicious accompaniment to almost any meal and are just the thing for serving up to guests. Perfect for when you have a glut of fresh lemons, too! This recipe was given to me years ago by fellow foodie friend, Kim Brooks – hence the name, and I've been making it ever since. In fact, it was one of the dishes I made for Gareth when we first met, in order to impress him. Suffice to say, it worked! Quick and easy to make and refreshingly different, they're a winner every time.

Serves 4

Ingredients:

4 large potatoes (or 8 medium), peeled and cut into quarters

1 cup water

½ cup olive oil

½ cup freshly squeezed lemon juice (approximately 3 lemons)

1 tbsp dried oregano

1 tbsp salt

¼ tsp freshly ground black pepper

Method:

Preheat your oven to 200C. Peel the potatoes and cut into quarters, then place them into a fairly deep metal roasting tray or pan, large enough to fit the potatoes in a single layer. You don't want your tray to be shallow, as the potatoes cook in a lot of liquid. If you don't have a suitable metal tray, you can use any type of oven proof dish, just be aware that the cooking time may be longer. Add the water, olive oil, lemon juice, oregano and salt and pepper to the tray and toss the potatoes in it until well coated. Bake, uncovered for around 50 minutes or until tender, turning the potatoes halfway so they brown evenly. Ideally, you want all that lovely lemony sauce to have reduced to almost nothing. If the liquid has all been absorbed before the potatoes are fully browned, add more water. If there is still too much liquid, continue cooking a little longer, until it has reduced more. Once cooked, remove from the oven and serve.

Entertaining

Lip-Smacking Miso Tofu

WHEAT/GLUTEN FREE   ALLIUM FREE

This is my absolute favourite way to serve tofu. These sumptuous little pillows of joy are literally lip-smacking, hence the name. Another reason I love to make this recipe is it's just so simple. I like to prepare the tofu in the morning and let it sit in the marinade all day until dinner time, but if you're short on time you can get away with marinating it for just 30 minutes and it is still delicious. You can serve these with rice, steamed vegetables, salad, or they even taste wonderful popped in a wrap.

Serves 2 - 4

Ingredients:

1 block firm tofu, drained and pressed

1 tbsp rice vinegar

2 tbsp tamari

2 tbsp olive oil

2 tbsp miso paste

Method:

First, drain and press the tofu and cut into smallish cubes – around half-inch. Put all the rest of the ingredients into a medium-sized bowl or container and mix well together. Add the tofu cubes to the container and mix well gently, to coat. Leave for at least 30 minutes, turning occasionally to coat further.

Once ready to cook, heat a large frying pan on medium-high heat and add in the tofu, as well as all the marinade from the container. You don't need to add any oil to the pan, the marinade will prevent it from sticking. Cook, turning regularly for around 8 – 10 minutes, until the tofu is well browned. Serve as desired.

Entertaining

Mum's Famous Flatbreads

CAN BE MADE

WHEAT/GLUTEN FREE   ALLIUM FREE

This easy, versatile recipe has helped us through many a tight week when the pantry and bank balance is bare, but just because they're cheap to make doesn't mean they're not special; quite the opposite. Gareth's mum, Christina is a real 'breadwinner' and has been making these for years for friends and family. A summer never passes without her being asked to take them along to gatherings to cook on the barbecue. You never lose the joy in the feeling and aroma of making your own home-made bread and this recipe is a great activity to do with young children, as well as invaluable teaching for older offspring to stand them in good stead for leaving home and surviving on a student budget.

The flatbread's list of uses is limited only by your imagination. Roll them extra thin to make tortillas or leave them thicker to make a delicious naan. Add rosemary and olive oil to make herb bread or cut leftover flatbread into triangles and bake in the oven to make pita chips. Tear them up and dunk them in dips or hummus or fold a whole one around a couple of slices of Dragon's Egg(plant) (page 125) to make a soft taco. You can also substitute regular flour for gluten-free flour, such as rice, to make them suitable for coeliacs. Have a go at making them for yourself and see how many other ideas you can come up with!

Makes 8 flatbreads

Ingredients:

2 cups plain or gluten-free flour

1 tsp salt

1 tbsp olive oil

⅔ cup warm water

extra flour, for dusting

Method:

Sift the flour into a large bowl and add the salt. In a separate small bowl or jug, add the oil to the warm water and whisk, then pour it gradually into the flour, stirring well with a metal spoon until you have a soft dough. Turn out on to a lightly floured work surface and begin kneading, adding a little more flour if the dough seems too sticky. Keep kneading for around five minutes, then make the dough into a ball and set aside to rest for at least 15 minutes before cooking.

Entertaining

Method Continued ...

Once you're ready to cook your flatbreads, roll your dough out into a sausage and divide it equally into eight pieces. Roll each piece into a ball, then roll out each ball on a floured surface, into a rough circle. Don't be scared to add plenty of flour to the surface, and to your rolling pin, to stop your flatbreads from sticking.

To cook, heat a large frying pan over a high heat. Once hot, reduce the heat to medium and carefully transfer one of the flatbreads into the pan. Leave to cook for a couple of minutes, until you can see the edges of the flatbread start to lift away from the pan. Using a large spatula, flip it over and cook the other side in the same way. Quickly remove from the pan and set aside while you repeat the process with the other flatbreads. You can help to keep your cooked flatbreads soft and warm while cooking the others by lining a plate with a clean tea towel and wrapping them up in a bundle until you have finished cooking. Serve immediately, while still warm.

Entertaining

Plant-Based Platter

Entertaining guests and impressing them with vegan food doesn't have to entail hours of slaving in the kitchen. Why not feed them a rainbow? A colourful platter is always admired and appreciated, and many everyday platter foods are already naturally vegan. Putting together an awesome, mouth-watering spread is as easy as chopping a few raw vegetables and opening a couple of jars. Here are some of our favourite ideas:

Ingredients:

fresh carrot, cucumber and celery, cut into sticks

hummus (bought or home-made, using our recipe on page 102)

plant based pesto

olives

pickled gherkins

fresh or pickled capsicum, sliced

asparagus spears

cherry tomatoes

sundried tomatoes

pickled artichoke hearts

whole baby beetroot

vegan feta, cut into bite-sized cubes and rubbed with olive oil and dried oregano

sauerkraut, or vegan kimchi

pickled onions

dairy-free cheese, cut into small slices, or cubed

crackers (we love seed crackers but you can use rice crackers, buckwheat, whatever you prefer)

chutney or farm style pickle

artisan bread, such as sourdough or ciabatta

flatbreads (e.g. Mum's Famous Flatbreads page 188)

small dish of olive or other flavoured oil, for dipping

Method:

Simply arrange all together on a large platter or plate, accompanied by small bowls as required and encourage everyone to dig in. It's so easy to enjoy a wide range of healthy, vegan foods without even trying!

Entertaining

Portomiso Burger

CAN BE MADE

WHEAT/GLUTEN FREE   GRAIN FREE   ALLIUM FREE

'Umami' is a term which is unfamiliar to many but is one of the five basic tastes, along with sweet, sour, salty and bitter. You can taste it in savoury vegan foods such as seaweed, miso and mushrooms and this recipe gives you a double whammy. We can't think of 'umami' without thinking of 'yummy' and this burger is very much both! A big, juicy portobello mushroom is just as satisfying and 'meaty' as any regular patty. If you've never tried it, you need to! Super easy to cook and rich in flavour without being too spicy, you can also enjoy the marinated mushroom without the bun, for a lighter, gluten-free meal of 'steak' and salad.

Serves 4

Ingredients:

4 large portobello mushrooms

2 tbsp sesame oil

2 tbsp chilli paste

2 tbsp miso paste

salt and freshly ground black pepper, to taste

4 burger buns

favourite burger toppings of choice

Method:

Wipe mushrooms gently with a paper towel to remove any dirt as necessary. Put the sesame oil, chilli paste and miso together in a bowl, with a scrunch of salt and pepper and mix until well combined. Using a brush or butter knife, baste the mushrooms all over on both sides with the spice paste. Set aside for 30 minutes, turning and basting again occasionally.

Once the mushrooms have finished marinating, heat a large, non-stick frying pan over medium heat. No extra oil should be required if you're using a non-stick pan, the marinade is juicy enough. Pop the mushrooms into the pan and cook around 5 - 8 minutes on both sides, turning as necessary, until they are tender and heated through. Remove and serve in buns with your favourite toppings, or on their own, with accompanying vegetables and/or salad.

Entertaining

Ratatouille

WHEAT/GLUTEN FREE   GRAIN FREE   ALLIUM FREE

This colourful dish brings back wonderful memories of my childhood. Every year, on November 5th we would have a huge neighbourhood get together for Mum's birthday and she would make an enormous pot of ratatouille for the grownups, while us youngsters tucked into baked potatoes, cooked in the bonfire embers. It took a few more years for me to develop an appreciation for this traditional Provençal vegetable stew but now it's a dish I often enjoy making for guests and get asked to take along to get-togethers. You can enjoy it hot or cold, as a main or side dish, with rice, baked potato or with fresh, crusty bread. For those who are intolerant to garlic like myself, you can actually leave it out and it still tastes delicious.

Just don't tell the French!

Serves 4

Ingredients:

6 tbsp olive oil

2 medium courgettes (zucchini), diced

1 large eggplant, cut into cubes

salt

1 whole red capsicum, diced

3 cloves garlic (optional)

1 x 400g can chopped tomatoes

1 tbsp tomato paste

1 tbsp chopped fresh thyme

½ tsp sugar

pinch chilli flakes

salt and freshly ground black pepper, to taste

Method:

Heat the olive oil in a large pan over medium heat. Add the diced courgettes to the pan and sauté for 5 minutes, stirring frequently. Remove from the pan and set aside. Sprinkle the diced eggplant liberally with salt, then also add to the pan. Reduce the heat and cook gently for 10 minutes, stirring frequently until the flesh is well-softened. Remove from the pan and set aside with the courgettes. Add the chopped capsicum, along with the garlic if you're using it, and cook another 5 minutes, then add in the tomatoes, tomato paste, thyme, sugar and chilli flakes and stir well. Return the eggplant and courgettes to the pan and bring to the boil. Reduce the heat and simmer for 10 minutes. Taste for seasoning, adding salt and pepper to taste. Serve as desired.

Entertaining

Roast Stuffages

WHEAT/GLUTEN FREE   ALLIUM FREE

Despite the outlandish name, these beauties taste surprisingly traditional. Think of an old-fashioned Sunday roast, but in the shape of a sausage! Each delicately crunchy bite conjures up memories of delicious herby stuffing, while being substantial enough to take the place of the usual meat, served alongside all the veggies. They also make a tasty sandwich filler when cold too, just like a regular roast!

NB: You don't **have** to use cling wrap if you don't want to, however it does play an essential part in helping the 'sausages' keep their shape. Just make sure you remember to remove it before cooking!

Serves 4

Ingredients:

1 ½ cups polenta (cornmeal flour)

3 cups vegan beef style stock

2 tbsp nutritional yeast

3 tsp fresh rosemary, finely chopped (or 2 tsp if you're using dried)

2 tsp sage

small amount oil, for brushing

Method:

Put the stock, nutritional yeast, rosemary and sage together in a large pot (we use a soup pot). Heat over a medium heat and bring to the boil. Once boiling, gradually add in the polenta with one hand, while all the time stirring briskly with the other. Continue beating the mixture until you end up with a very thick mass of polenta, similar to stuffing consistency. Remove from the heat.

Line an 20cm x 20cm (8"x 8") baking dish or similar size with cling wrap. Scrape out all the polenta into the dish. Spread and smooth it all out as best you can until it covers the whole dish. Set aside for 10 minutes, to cool slightly.

While the mixture is cooling, cut 10 small rectangles of cling wrap, approximately 30cm x 18cm in size. This part can be a

Entertaining

Method Continued ...

bit fiddly; if you can get someone to help you by holding the roll of cling wrap taut while you cut it, it makes the process a lot quicker! If you prefer, you can just form your sausages freehand, without wrapping, but the cling wrap does really help them to keep their shape better and stop the mixture from spreading during cooking.

Once your mixture is cool enough to handle, cut it into 10 equal finger pieces. Remove each piece one at a time and place it onto one of the pieces of cling wrap, near the edge. Pick up the edge and begin rolling the mixture over, making a sausage shape as you go and encasing it in a 'tube' of cling wrap. Using your index finger and thumb, pinch the ends of the tube and twist several times, to create an airtight sausage casing. Tuck the ends neatly underneath before placing your finished sausage back into the dish, with the tucked ends facing down to help keep the sausage watertight and in shape. When all the sausages have been made, pop them into the refrigerator to chill for at least an hour.

To finish cooking, preheat the oven to 220C. Remove all the sausages from their cling wrap and brush with a little oil. Bake for 30 minutes, then turn over and bake for another 10 minutes. Remove from the oven and serve.

Entertaining

Undercover Vegan Lasagne

CAN BE MADE

WHEAT/GLUTEN FREE

This is a recipe our family has been making and enjoying for a long time, first as a vegetarian dish, then adapted to make it vegan. Despite being a farmer for many years, I was vegetarian for most of them and I'll never forget taking this lasagne to a pot luck dinner. Every person in the room was either a dairy or beef farmer and I was afraid I would get teased mercilessly as soon as they discovered there was no meat in their lasagne; yet not one of these burly blokes realised. In fact, they couldn't stop saying how good it was and all of them went back for seconds! The sauce is so rich and flavoursome, even kids don't notice they're eating spinach, courgette and all sorts of other things they would normally turn their noses up at, making it the perfect family dish. Don't be put off by the long list of ingredients, it's really not hard. You throw most of it in one pot and forget about it for a good part of the time! To make your lasagne gluten-free, simply use gluten-free pasta sheets instead of regular and gluten-free flour in place of regular white flour.

Serves 6 – 8

Ingredients:

¼ cup water

1 large onion, finely chopped

2 cloves garlic, finely chopped or crushed

2 medium-sized carrots, grated

2 courgettes (zucchini), chopped

1 whole red or green capsicum, chopped

3 – 4 medium button mushrooms, sliced

2 cups chopped spinach or silver beet

1 x 400g can tomato puree

1 x 400g can chopped tomatoes in juice

1 ½ cups water

1 tbsp brown sugar

1 tbsp dried basil

2 tsp dried mixed herbs

3 tbsp fresh parsley, chopped finely

salt and freshly ground black pepper, to taste

White Sauce:

3 tbsp dairy-free spread

6 tbsp plain flour (you can also use gluten-free flour, such as rice flour)

3 cups soy milk (you can use almond if that's all you have but soy milk gives a

Entertaining

White Sauce Continued

much better and more authentic flavour)

400g (approximately) regular or gluten-free lasagne pasta, you can use fresh or dried

1 cup dairy-free cheese, grated – or more, to taste, for topping

Method:

Heat the quarter-cup of water in a large pan over medium heat. Add the onion, garlic and grated carrot to the pan and cook for 5 minutes, stirring occasionally, until the vegetables are soft. Add in the courgettes, capsicum, mushrooms and spinach or silverbeet, followed by the tomato puree, tinned tomatoes and water. Sprinkle in the brown sugar, dried herbs and parsley and stir everything together well. Bring to the boil, then reduce the heat to low and simmer gently for one hour. Once cooked, season to taste with salt and freshly ground black pepper.

While the sauce is cooking, you can get on to making your white sauce. In a medium-sized saucepan, heat the dairy-free spread over medium-high heat until melted. Add the flour, stirring briskly for a minute or so to combine with the spread (don't worry if it goes all strange and lumpy, you're going to thin it down in a tick!) then gradually add in the soy milk, stirring all the time until you have a thick, smooth sauce. Once you've added in all the milk and beaten the sauce until there are no lumps, remove it from the heat and set aside until ready to use.

To put the lasagne together, grease a 30cm x 20cm baking dish, or similar large baking dish, around 5cm deep. Spread a little of your cooked vegetable sauce on the base, then cover the bottom with some of the pasta sheets. Cover that with 2 – 3 cups more of the vegetable sauce, then repeat with more pasta, more sauce and so on, ending with the pasta. Pour your white sauce across the top, smoothing over so that it reaches all the corners, and finish with the grated cheese, being careful not to overfill the dish.

Preheat the oven for 10 minutes at 160C, then pop in the lasagne and cook for 45 – 50 minutes, until the cheese is golden and melted and the pasta is cooked right the way through when you test it with a sharp knife. Remove from the oven and leave to 'rest' for 10 – 15 minutes before serving. Enjoy with a fresh salad and crusty bread.

Entertaining

Vegetable Kabobs

These flavoursome fellas are brilliant to take along to a BBQ or just enjoy for an easy summertime dinner. We have found the easiest way (not to mention the tastiest) is to prepare and marinade your vegies first, before threading them onto the skewers, rather than try and coat them properly once they're on the skewers. It allows for far better coverage and really enables the flavours to soak into the vegetables. We've served these up at many a BBQ and our non-vegan friends always love them too, nobody misses the meat!

Serves 4

Ingredients:

You can use more or less of any of the following
2 cups mushrooms

1 cup cherry tomatoes

1 red capsicum, cut into large chunks

1 green capsicum, cut into large chunks

1 red onion, cut into chunks

1 - 2 courgettes (zucchini), cut into thick slices

1 sweetcorn cob, husk removed and cut into slices

bamboo or metal BBQ skewers

Marinade
½ cup olive oil

3 cloves garlic, crushed or finely chopped

Juice of 1 lemon (or more, to taste)

1 tsp dried oregano

1 tsp dried basil
Plenty of salt and freshly ground black pepper

Method:

Put the olive oil, garlic, lemon juice, oregano and basil into a small bowl and season well with salt and pepper.

Put all of the prepared vegetables into a large container or bowl. Pour over the marinade and mix well, using your hands to coat the vegetables thoroughly. Cover and/or refrigerate and leave for at least four hours, or even overnight to allow the flavours to develop.

Once marinated, thread the vegetables alternately onto the skewers in an attractive rotation of colours and flavours and put onto a baking tray. To cook, either barbecue, turning occasionally until the vegetables are tender, or you can roast in the oven. Serve immediately.

Entertaining

Sauces, Dressings & Gravies

One of the biggest discoveries we made when we became vegan, was that the secret to incredible tasting food had not been in the meat, dairy or eggs, the way we had always believed. It was the sauce, the seasonings, the herbs and spices who were responsible the whole time! Gorgeous, glossy gravies, creamy, dreamy dressings and mind-blowing sauces all abound in vegan cooking. Often all it takes is something as simple as a teaspoon or two of something different, stirred into a plain vegan mayo to turn an everyday dinner into a fine dining affair. It's these beloved flavours which make a dish unforgettable and make you want to make them again and again. The following only take only a short time to make and devour, but your taste buds and memories will want to hold onto them a lot longer!

Creamy Mushroom Gravy

WHEAT/GLUTEN FREE   ALLIUM FREE

This gravy is so rich tasting and full of mushroom-y goodness! Just the thing for spooning generously over oven-baked potatoes, to turn ordinary mashed spuds into something decadent or to accompany vegan sausages and veggies. Pure comfort food at its best, and quick to make too!

Serves 4

Ingredients:

2 ½ tbsp olive oil

250g mushrooms, sliced

200ml coconut cream

1 tbsp tamari

1 ½ tbsp Worcestershire sauce (check to make sure it is vegan and doesn't contain fish)

1 tbsp fresh parsley, finely chopped

1 tbsp cornflour

¼ cup water salt and freshly ground black pepper, to taste

Method:

Heat the olive oil in a medium-sized pan, over medium heat. Add the sliced mushrooms and cook gently for five minutes, stirring occasionally. Add the coconut cream, tamari, Worcestershire sauce and parsley to the pan and stir well to combine. Bring to the boil, then reduce heat to low and simmer for five minutes. In a separate small bowl or cup, mix the tablespoon of cornflour with the water until smooth. Gradually add it to the pan, stirring all the time, until the gravy becomes thick and glossy. Remove from the heat and serve.

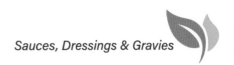

Sauces, Dressings & Gravies

Dijon Mayo

WHEAT/GLUTEN FREE   ALLIUM FREE

Just a small amount of Dijon mustard it all it takes to give a nice, mild tang and a bit of a special touch to regular mayonnaise. Slather it on your burger buns when building a vegan burger and you'll never want to go back!

Serves 2 - 4

Ingredients:

1 tbsp vegan mayonnaise

1 tsp Dijon mustard

Method:

Put the mayonnaise into a small bowl and add the teaspoon of mustard. Using a spoon, stir briskly until smooth.

Sauces, Dressings & Gravies

Green Sauce

WHEAT/GLUTEN FREE · GRAIN FREE · ALLIUM FREE

We racked our brains for a suitably prestigious name for this amazing sauce, as it is most deserving of one, but it's always been just 'Green Sauce' to us, for obvious reasons! The flavour is as intense as its colour, with the nutritional yeast providing a nice 'bite' to the sauce, while the jalapeños give it a lovely tang and a bit of a kick, but not too much. We love to serve this sauce up on special occasions but it makes a terrific accompaniment to anything from potato wedges and roast potatoes to salads and is perfect for jazzing up everyday lunch wraps.

Makes approximately one cup

Ingredients:

1 cup spinach leaves

1 cup fresh coriander (cilantro)

¼ cup jalapeños

3 tbsp pumpkin seeds (or you could use sunflower seeds, or pine nuts)

2 tbsp nutritional yeast

2 tbsp lime juice

3 tbsp olive oil

¼ cup water, or more, as needed

Salt, to taste

Method:

Put all the ingredients except the salt into a medium-sized bowl or jug. Using a stick blender (or you can just use a regular blender), whiz everything up until you have a smooth, green sauce. If it's too thick you can add more water, just a splash at a time, until you reach the desired consistency. Taste for seasoning, adding salt as necessary.

Sauces, Dressings & Gravies

Hot Mustard Dressing

WHEAT/GLUTEN FREE **GRAIN FREE** **ALLIUM FREE**

Before reaching for your everyday whole-seed or Dijon, have a go at making this fast and easy dressing to add some extra zing to your meals. It is Gareth's very favourite and if he could, he would have it on everything. Discover the joy of hot mustard!

Serves 2 - 4

Ingredients:

2 tbsp olive oil

1 tbsp balsamic vinegar

1 tsp sesame oil

1 tsp maple syrup

1 tsp hot mustard

Method:

Put all the ingredients together in a small bowl or jug and stir thoroughly until the dressing is completely smooth and well combined. Once made, keeps well covered in the refrigerator for several days.

Sauces, Dressings & Gravies

Impossibly Rich Herby Gravy

OIL FREE   WHEAT/GLUTEN FREE   ALLIUM FREE

A really good gravy can be hard to find, when it comes to feeding both vegans and non-vegans alike. How on earth do you possibly make a rich, flavourful 'proper' gravy out of nothing but plants? With this recipe, that's how! It never lets us down and always leaves everyone at the table full to the brim and smiling. It makes around three cups of delicious gravy, so plenty to go around and is perfect poured liberally over Neatballs (page 137) and mash.

Serves 4 - 6

Ingredients:

3 cups vegetable stock

⅓ cup tamari

3 tsp Worcestershire sauce (check first to make sure it's vegan)

1 tsp fresh parsley

¾ tsp dried thyme

¾ tsp dried sage

1 tsp smoked paprika

large pinch freshly ground black pepper

To thicken:

5 tbsp cornflour

½ cup water

Method:

Put the vegetable stock into a large saucepan over medium heat. Add the tamari, Worcestershire sauce, parsley, thyme, sage, smoked paprika and black pepper to the stock and mix all together well. Bring to the boil, then reduce the heat and simmer for 5 minutes. Remove from the heat.

In a small jug, mix the cornflour and water together until you have a smooth, runny paste. Then slowly – slowly! - pour the paste into the pan of gravy, stirring all the time to reduce the chance of lumps. Your gravy should instantly start to thicken. Put the pan back onto the heat and let simmer gently for another 2 – 3 minutes, stirring all the time. Serve while hot.

Lemon Tahini Dressing

OIL FREE   WHEAT/GLUTEN FREE   GRAIN FREE   ALLIUM FREE

I make this simple dressing all the time to drizzle over my salads. It's creamy, but not too thick and goes with pretty much everything. You can add more cayenne if you want to make it a little spicy.

Serves 2 - 4

Ingredients:

⅓ cup water

¼ cup lemon juice

⅓ cup tahini

½ tsp ground cumin

small pinch cayenne pepper

¼ tsp salt

Method:

Put all the ingredients into a medium bowl or jug and blitz using a stick blender until smooth. Keeps well for several days in the refrigerator, in an airtight container.

Sauces, Dressings & Gravies

Miso Gravy

OIL FREE   WHEAT/GLUTEN FREE   ALLIUM FREE

One of the many things people think they are going to miss out on when going vegan, is no longer being able to enjoy proper gravy. Being gravy lovers ourselves, we also envisaged this being a problem. We were overjoyed to learn however that real, proper, delicious gravy is very much still possible. This rich, glossy gravy is fast and easy to make and tops off any meal from vegan sausages and mash to a full-blown roast dinner with all the trimmings. Whoever imagined vegan gravy could be so good?

Serves 4 - 6

Ingredients:

2 ½ cups vegetable stock

2 tbsp miso paste

1 tbsp tamari

1 tbsp nutritional yeast

¼ tsp black pepper

4 tbsp cornflour

½ cup water

Method:

Put the vegetable stock and miso paste into a saucepan over medium heat. Add the tamari, nutritional yeast and black pepper and mix well to dissolve the miso. Bring to the boil, then reduce the heat and simmer for five minutes. In a separate bowl or jug, put in the cornflour, followed by the half a cup of water. Stir briskly until smooth. Gradually add to the pan of miso gravy, stirring all the time to remove any lumps, until the gravy is thick and glossy. Remove from the heat and serve.

Sauces, Dressings & Gravies

Pico de Gallo

OIL FREE   WHEAT/GLUTEN FREE   GRAIN FREE

This typical Mexican tomato-based salsa is fresh and chunky enough to be a salad in its own right in our opinion, but we'd better not argue with generations of tradition. The perfect quick summer throw-together when you have an abundance of tomatoes, it's great as a party appetiser, or a snack with pita chips and guacamole. Plus of course you can pile it on all your favourite Mexican dishes, such as enchiladas, nachos and tacos! While you can whip it up in minutes, I like to rest the Pico de Gallo for a while if possible, to give the vegetables the time to exude all their tasty juice and enhance the flavour.

Serves 4 - 6

Ingredients:

5 large tomatoes, diced (I like to remove the seeds, but you don't have to)

1 red onion, finely chopped

1 jalapeño, finely chopped

½ cup fresh coriander (cilantro), chopped

2 tsp lime juice

Salt, to taste

Method:

Prepare the tomatoes, red onion, jalapeño and coriander. Put them all together in a large bowl, along with the coriander and lime juice. Gently toss all the ingredients together until well combined. Season to taste with freshly ground salt.

Sauces, Dressings & Gravies

SOS (Save Our Salad) Dressing

WHEAT/GLUTEN FREE

If you don't enjoy salads, like I used to, this simple dressing will change your life. From the moment I left home, I detested making salads, to the extent I pretty much stopped bothering, as they never tasted of anything. As I now thankfully know, the secret to an amazing salad lies in having a really good dressing. I've been making this one for years now and it still brings me joy. The flavour is essentially Asian but it goes well with pretty much any kind of leafy or tomato based salad and will rescue it from being boring!

Serves 4

Ingredients:

¼ cup tamari

¼ cup sweet chilli sauce

2 tsp rice vinegar

1 tsp sesame oil

1 ½ tbsp lemon juice
(I definitely recommend using fresh lemon juice here, or at very least the really good bottled stuff, otherwise it just won't taste the same)

Method:

Put all the ingredients into a clean container or bottle and shake well to combine. Drizzle over salads as required. When not using, store in the fridge and shake before using. Keeps well refrigerated.

Sriracha Mayo

WHEAT/GLUTEN FREE

Jazzing up a plain mayonnaise is so easy and instantly turns an everyday dish into something special. No need to splash out on expensive ready-made bottles when you can make your own at home! This sriracha mayo takes less than two minutes to put together and is every bit as good.

Serves 2 - 4

Ingredients:

¼ cup vegan mayonnaise

¼ cup sriracha

Method:

Put the mayonnaise in a small bowl with the sriracha sauce. Using a spoon, mix together until smooth. That's it!

Sauces, Dressings & Gravies

Tahini Miso Dressing

OIL FREE   WHEAT/GLUTEN FREE   ALLIUM FREE

Once you try this dressing, you will want to have it on literally everything and even eat it straight off the spoon. Gloriously rich and super-fast to make, you can either enjoy it as a creamy dressing to pour over salads, or as a dip for raw veggies, if you add less water.

Serves 2 - 4

Ingredients:

¼ cup tahini

1 tbsp lemon juice

1 tbsp tamari

1 tbsp miso paste

pinch chilli flakes

water, quantity as required, for mixing

Method:

Put the tahini, lemon juice, tamari, miso and chilli flakes into a small bowl or jug and stir all together into a paste until well combined. Add water, a little at a time, mixing well with each addition as you go, until smooth and you reach the desired consistency. We like ours fairly runny, for drizzling over salads but just keep mixing and tasting until you get a blend you like.

Undressing

WHEAT/GLUTEN FREE **ALLIUM FREE**

Despite the suggestive name, there is nothing mildly subtle or seductive about this one. We called it an 'undressing' because it knocks your socks off, pure and simple. But it's so wonderful at the same time, particularly with avocado! This recipe makes a smallish amount, which is most likely all you need, but you can of course double to make more.

Serves 2 - 4

Ingredients:

1 tbsp tamari

½ tbsp rice vinegar

½ tbsp olive oil

1 tsp wasabi paste

Method:

Put in the tamari into a small bowl, followed by the rice vinegar, olive oil, and wasabi paste. Mix thoroughly until smooth, making sure there are no lumps as you go (or you might get more than you bargained for when you take a mouthful!) Drizzle sparingly over salad – you can always go back for more!

Sauces, Dressings & Gravies

Wasabi Wrecking Ball Dressing

WHEAT/GLUTEN FREE   ALLIUM FREE

Despite its harmless looking appearance, this rather plain-looking dressing packs a powerful punch, hence the name. It takes only a couple of minutes to whip up and makes a nice, generous amount to last several days' worth of salads. We love this particularly on our Welsh Dragon Bowl (page 78) but you can use it to give any plain or Asian style salad a whole heap of zing!

Serves 2

Ingredients:

1 tsp fresh ginger, peeled and chopped

3 tbsp water

1 tbsp tamari

1 tbsp rice vinegar

2 ½ tbsp tahini

1 tsp sesame oil

2 tsp wasabi paste

1 tsp date syrup (or you could use maple)

Method:

Put all the ingredients together in a bowl or jug. Using a stick blender or regular blender, whizz everything up for 30 – 60 seconds, until completely smooth. Serve over salad.

Sauces, Dressings & Gravies

Wasabi Mayo

WHEAT/GLUTEN FREE   ALLIUM FREE

This has to be our favourite of all the flavoured mayo's. So sumptuous and creamy! Not to mention a splendid whack of that infamous Wasabi heat. Don't panic however; this easy recipe still gives you a decent amount of control. Test as you go, you can always add more, but not less! This versatile condiment is delicious on salads or baked potatoes, with potato wedges or polenta fries, with crispy tofu or even spread on a burger.

Serves 2 - 4

Ingredients:

¼ cup vegan mayonnaise

1 tsp Wasabi paste (or more, to taste)

Method:

Put the mayonnaise in a small bowl and add the teaspoon of Wasabi. Using a spoon, stir briskly until smooth with no lumps. Have a small taste. You may find this gives an adequate flavour and amount of heat, otherwise you can add more Wasabi paste if you prefer it stronger. Add just a tiny amount at a time, stirring well with each addition, until you reach the desired taste.

Sauces, Dressings & Gravies

Index

First published in 2020 by New Holland Publishers
Sydney • Auckland

Level 1, 178 Fox Valley Road, Wahroonga 2076, Australia
5/39 Woodside Ave, Northcote, Auckland 0627, New Zealand
newhollandpublishers.com

A record of this book is held at the National Library of Australia and New Zealand.

ISBN 9781760791414

Group Managing Director: Fiona Schultz
Publisher: David Brash
Project Editor: Xavier Waterkeyn
Designer: Yolanda La Gorcé
Production Director: Arlene Gippert

Printer: Toppan Leefung Printing Limited

10 9 8 7 6 5 4 3 2 1

Keep up with New Holland Publishers:

NewHollandPublishers

@newhollandpublishers

US $24.99